The Practice and Preaching of Liberation

THE PRACTICE AND PREACHING OF LIBERATION

William J. Nottingham

CBP Press
St. Louis, Missouri

Address: CBP Press
Box 179
St. Louis, MO 63166

Library of Congress Cataloging in Publication Data

Nottingham, William J.
The practice and preaching of liberation.

1. Liberation theology. 2. Preaching. I. Title.
BT83.57.N68 1986 230 85-18997
ISBN 0-8272-2931-3

Printed in the United States of America

Dedicated in love and gratitude
to my parents
Jess W. and Alice Green Nottingham
Sharon, Pennsylvania

Contents

Foreword

This is a *conservative* book. It calls Christians back to the roots of their faith in the Bible and in Jesus Christ.

This is a *radical* book. It challenges the assumptions of most American Christians. It compels us to think about our task as Christians in ways appropriate to the late twentieth century, ways that differ markedly from what was acceptable a generation ago. It forces us to broaden our vision to include the whole inhabited world, not just people who live near us and think as we do.

William J. Nottingham has skillfully transcended the spurious divisions that characterize so much contemporary Christianity. Does the Christian seek a personal relationship with Jesus Christ or the transformation of society as a whole? The Christian must seek both of these. Is preaching based on the Bible or on the latest news from Central America? Faithful preaching must be related to both. Is Christianity a matter of instant conversion, or is it a lifelong process of growth? It is both. Is the church an organized institution or a gathered community of those who acknowledge Christ as Lord? It is both.

Out of his rich personal experience, Dr. Nottingham develops a theology of preaching that is relevant to today's situation. After pondering the teachings of Reinhold Niebuhr and Paul Tillich at Union Theological Seminary, Nottingham spent several years in Europe, seeking to relate the gospel to the lives of persons recovering from the devastation and despair of war. Later, as a mission executive, he visited many countries on every continent. He served as an executive for Latin America and the Caribbean, for East Asia and the Pacific, and finally for the whole overseas mission of his denomination. Through wide reading and personal contacts, he has sought to understand the faith of Third World theologians and the peoples for whom they speak.

In this book, Nottingham brings what he has learned in his extensive travels home to his native United States. He calls Christians and their pastors to think in terms of *liberation*, not just for the Third World, but for the church and its members in the USA.

Here he spells out what it means to set persons free from outworn concepts and from oppressive social structures. He calls for a rediscovery of the gospel that speaks both to the social and to the personal aspects of human life. He calls for a realism that accepts the inevitability of failure in every human endeavor, and at the same time he preaches faith in the possibility of a renewed society under God's rule. The Christian mission, he writes, is about "how we may find blessing and liberation, a means to resist evil and to witness to true humanity, and the spiritual strength to sustain losses while still seeking change."

Herbert H. Lambert
Editor, CBP Press

1
Why Preach for Liberation?

Jesus Christ is the head of the church and the only issue in all its preaching. He is its source and its life. The question for Christian theology today is how he shapes our awareness of God. From this awareness flow faith, hope, and love, which have a bearing on our self-understanding, our relationships with one another, and our actions in the world. The Bible, the liturgical tradition, the mystical legacy, and the theological formulations of many centuries leave no room to argue otherwise. Jesus Christ is the issue for preaching. The way he is interpreted shows what we understand to be God's will and purpose for our lives.

This is why liberation becomes a theme in preaching. It is not possible to shut our minds to the meaning Jesus has for the poor and exploited who have set the seal of "liberation " on this generation. To say that Jesus Christ is Lord and Savior is utterly meaningless if it ignores the implications of the 700 billion dollars spent on the arms race in 1985! It is a moral and spiritual anomaly for American Christians to find comfort and inspiration through the Holy Spirit and to forget the hungry millions of their own society and across the world or the almost trillion dollar indebtedness of the so-called Third World to the so-called rich world. To learn of the Mothers of the Plaza de Mayo in Buenos Aires, who demonstrate every Thursday for their loved ones tortured and murdered under military dictatorship from 1976 to 1983, is to discover new meaning in the protest of the cross. The violation of human rights in the U.S.S.R. or Afghanistan, and the killings in El Salvador, Guatemala, and Nicaragua,through the involvement of our own country, raises the importance of the unity of the church around the world and the relationships of world mission. The preaching of Good News is relevant to what is actually happening in the world, where there is so much bad news. Because Jesus Christ is the issue for preaching, God's judgment and compassion for our world today are revealed in an unmistakable way.

Deliverance is the action and concern of God both in the Old Testament and in the New—the perception of grace and the signs of the kingdom of justice and peace that is to be. The preoccupation of the world today with liberation and its suppression or exploitation has deep religious meaning. It is a spiritual movement having the momentum of faith. Religion speaks of "salvation" as the ultimate liberation that reaches us from beyond every contingency of life, like the kingdom of God in all its fullness. But what is visible in obedience and service, the necessary conversion or transformation of life, is "redemption," the freeing from sin and the freeing of slaves. *Liberation* is a proper translation of redemption; it describes the experience of freedom that applies to our world today. It points to the judgment of God and the question of God's manifestation in the world of the twentieth century, for liberation is a sign of what God does in bringing life from death.

Liberating Both Individuals and Society

To understand and communicate the gospel today, we must take "liberation theology" seriously. It is helping us to see the global and the true context of our lives. Not only is it pointing to political and economic structures that are oppressive, but it also shows our need to analyze our own relation to such structures, as social classes and as individuals. In our most intimate conflicts and difficulties, those to which pastoral counseling is addressed, it is not only the individual who needs help. In his remarkable book *Moral Man and Immoral Society* (1936), Reinhold Niebuhr wrote, "Society, in fact, conspired the cross."[1] This is still the case. The gospel of God's grace in Jesus Christ does not simply provide a means of adjustment and of finding things "okay"; it also proclaims judgment on the forces that move and shape us. How we may find blessing and liberation, a means to resist evil and to witness to true humanity, and the spiritual strength to sustain repeated losses while still seeking change—this is precisely the nature of Christian mission in our society today.

An illustration may be drawn from a well-known prayer of Dr. Niebuhr. It has been erroneously attributed to St. Francis, St. Augustine, the sages of India, and the philosophers of ancient Greece. It has been adopted as the official prayer of Alcoholics Anonymous. It is found in souvenir shops all over the world. Niebuhr composed it for a simple church service about fifty years ago.[2] The prayer corresponds remarkably to the personal needs of this past half-century, when acceptance of reality was a necessary theme for psychological and theological concern:

> God grant me
> The serenity to accept the things I cannot change,
> The courage to change the things I can,
> And the wisdom to know the difference.

Today, Niebuhr himself might want to revise the prayer in order to deal more adequately with the current situation. He might add a fourth request: "And the insight to know why." With such insight, the most common obstacles to change would be clear to us: structural power and social pressures which masquerade as "the inevitable nature of things." Perhaps, like the people of an earlier age, we would then be able to name the demon and exorcise it. We might gain control over our own lives.

It is possible to find serenity, courage, and wisdom, but have no awareness of why things are the way they are or what it would take to change some of them. Some of our most serious personal problems—alcoholism, family disputes, vocational maladjustment, poverty—are not merely the fault of individual limitations, but of value systems and subtle social tensions that arise from structures of profit and power.

The problems of teenagers or of the aging are not due to the weakness of individuals only, but are partly the result of the exploitative subcultures to which persons are exposed in the average American high school and in the typical urban environment. Serenity and courage, in such environments, need to take account of the kind of world in which we live and of the simple fact of human mortality. The gospel enables us to know not only that the cross of Christ is a victory but also what kind of victory it is. As a Thai student has said, "in a hopeless situation, we do have a little hope."

In contemporary society, the importance of the gospel must be stated in terms different from those used a generation ago. Paul Tillich and other existentialists found in the human "search for meaning" the point of contact between the gospel and persons. But meaning does not seem to be a major concern today. People do find meaning in many things. But in a larger world that does not share one's own views, meaning can represent false security and seem like a temporary escape mechanism. Sometimes private meaning is abstracted from the sufferings and oppression that support the life style of the one finding contentment with his or her meaning. We are tempted to ignore the judgment of God in the crisis of the poor. Here is a spiritual dilemma of tremendous consequence for us all!

Finding Life Worthwhile

The basic human problem today does not concern meaning, but worth or worthwhileness. The need for a sense of personal worth leads educators and counselors to emphasize affirmation and assertiveness. Questions are asked about the worth of human effort, about the value of one's life work, and even about living itself. Tillich said that we feel the need and hear the call of unambiguous life in the midst of ambiguity. Today, not only is life ambiguous, but the ambiguity is cumulative. As our horizons become vastly enlarged, ambiguity multiplies. The flower children of the 1960s came at the end of our search for meaning. The economic and ecological pessimism of the 1970s, viewed against the background of Vietnam and our relations with the Third World, made any particular "meaning" seem relative and petty. Perhaps concern about death can be handled by a people who have "come of age." Whether we can deal with *life* is the real question. The death wish is sometimes stronger than the life wish. Millions share a sense of futility, a deep despair like that behind the tragedy of Jonestown. In spite of the opportunities, freedom, and material advantages of American life, there are many lonely people among us. What they think and do doesn't seem to matter. They apparently can't affect the course of events, and this leads them to ask whether their contribution and concern over a whole lifetime is worth anything at all.

The gospel must be brought into sharp contrast with this view of reality, not because it offers a rosier picture, but because it affirms the struggle, courage, and sense of worth within the apparent hopelessness all about us. The message of the cross is not a success story about a "winning team." It is the source of assurance and trust that can give us serenity without passivity and courage to push for change without false hopes.

Balancing Hope and Realism

Phan Boi Chau, nationalist revolutionary in Vietnam before World War I, wrote from prison about the tragic nature of his struggle against the French colonialists: "I tried to patch up the sky and fill in the ocean."[3] Some struggles are, in fact, overwhelming. But his view of the struggle was not that of an idealist; he saw the sufferings of his people in flesh and blood. Not only were their national honor and cultural dignity thrust aside by French cannons and bayonets, but also a form of slavery was imposed to produce rubber and other raw materials for France. It was racist, brutal, and cruel—literally a dehumanizing of persons for the sake of economic profit and world markets. Imprisoned from 1914 to 1917, Chau could neither renounce his critical judgment and opposition nor see any practical solution. It was like "patching up the sky."

People in Asia, Africa, and Latin America suffer the same kinds of injustice today. Can Americans avoid sharing in their sorrow and frustration? To respond adequately to such suffering we must analyze the power structures, and have a clear perception of the world in which we live. This will provide a basis for moral and spiritual solidarity that is not just sentimental but has some political relevance.

The gospel can keep us from shutting our eyes to this sad reality and at the same time give us a ground of hope that is objective and ultimately universal. It can save us from naively thinking we can do much to help, but also from cynically disregarding our obligation. Christ is important to the world because we cannot relate to the Third World on the basis of our own righteousness, good will, and good deeds. There is a spiritual reality involved: forgiveness, openness to new solutions, and hope that is not dependent on our own intensity and achievement. Today, justification by faith means more than the overcoming of guilt in our search for God and for salvation. It means overcoming guilt in relations among races and economic classes. It means overcoming guilt in the domination of the Third World by a handful of rich countries.

It would be encouraging to be able to say that Phan Boi Chau could hope in a liberation that he would not live to see but one which would finally occur. In a sense this is true, but the suffering and ambivalence in Vietnam show that, even after victory, new problems arise in a society still largely dominated by the great powers. Trying to correct this is like "filling in the ocean," and a person's heart and mind can be overwhelmed by the task.

Because we trust in the power of Christ to overcome sin and death, we can hope for success in the people's struggle in Eastern Europe, the Philippines, or Chile, and we can ally ourselves with a creative and enduring force that condemns injustice, unrighteousness, and the oppression of the poor. This does not mean that we can try to "patch up the sky and fill in the ocean" with a new surge of idealism and self-generated confidence. It means that, in order to work for change, we must learn the political nature of certain problems and the special role we have within them. It means that we do not depend on our own subjectivity, but on the material reality around us and on the historical nature of the cross, interpreted through our subjectivity and within the believing community. We are related to one another through Jesus Christ and his church. We do not invent anything, but we offer our own specific contribution, wherever we are. The struggle and the outcome are products of history and of the Spirit, and they will use us more than we will use them.

The church can and should be the foremost place in which to link up with the larger struggle and to protest against evil while realizing that the struggle never ends. Victory is mediated by the love and sufferings of others, but (as we see in the cross) a mediated victory is given not only from the present, with its trust and commitment, but also from the *future*, which it reflects in the form of hope. The mediated victory, or liberation through grace, does not lessen the struggle for material change, as we see when the disciples get themselves organized after Pentecost. A mediated victory keeps any struggle for justice from appearing final, on the one hand, or too costly, on the other. It does not leave the affluent with a good conscience, but with an awakened consciousness. Nothing anyone can do is enough, but we can always be free enough to do more than we do. A sense of guilt is not what is needed, but it points to a solution and must be dealt with in the context of atonement and of the reality of God. God's blessing can be known to the extent that it is shared somehow with others.

Because it resurrects the human spirit, the gospel has special importance in the contemporary world. The church serves a power of love and justice that transcends the possibilities of history and therefore cannot be defeated by the limitations and frustrations of history. The realism of the gospel is that historical structures of power are *not* unchangeable. It is proclaimed in a community that is not bound by history, one that can endure the long and complicated struggles for goals that remain unrealized, giving a sense of worthwhileness to the lonely and partial role of the individual and of his or her immediate group.

The Urgency of Preaching the Gospel

Does this seem a long way from the sermon delivered on Sunday morning? It is not. If the sermon is considered to be one of the main ways in which the central message of the church is communicated, the above is not unrelated to it. The central message is the gospel, which to the ultimate limits of their sensibilities has relevance for people's sense of worth. If the church has such a message, and this is for all of us to decide for ourselves, it is urgent that the message be articulated, specified, elaborated, illustrated, considered prayerfully, and proclaimed as the good news of God.

If this is not the good news that some people want to hear, especially because it is good news for the poor and the poor in spirit, that only proves that the preacher has a missionary task. When his or her opportunity comes to tell what God has done in Jesus Christ and to proclaim, argue, or teach what that implies for the whole life of the people listening, there is a new moment in the mission of God for the salvation of humankind and for the transformation of the world in both big and little ways.

If we are to pray "Thy kingdom come," baptize in the name of the Father, Son, and Holy Spirit, celebrate the faith of Christmas and Easter, and sing of repentance and resurrection, we must not only ask what these actions should mean for Christians in the 1980s but also recognize that to a large extent they have been sapped of meaning and almost totally distorted by the provincial attitudes that prevail all about us. Christian doctrine has acquired false and alien meanings more often associated with our sense of well-being than with our passionate concern for one another. The evidence for this is in the experience of every thoughtful minister. It accounts for the disaffection of many people who have turned from the church either because it does not challenge their secularized existence or because they think and care about God and about our home in the creation more than their religious leaders do.

The mission of the church makes the sermon a vital part of the minister's task and of the faith community's service to God and to all people. It is the only way people can understand what God has suffered and is suffering for them. It is the only way they can learn what is expected of them as human beings and what is offered to them in the Spirit. The church may be the only place in which persons hear the whole truth about their own situation. It may be the only place where they hear described the larger life and joy that Christian faith, prayer, and solidarity with the whole world make possible to them. The church is certainly the one reminder of a transcendent judgment on our national life that is both terrible in its possible consequences and mercifully redemptive in its call for humane alternatives.

Notes

2

The Bible and Liberation Preaching

The preacher's function is to serve the word of God: *verbi divini minister*. He or she is, in the Protestant tradition, "servant of the divine word."

There are multiple ministries in the church, and the Spirit and the word underlie all of them. From apostolic times there have been a variety of callings, gifts, and offices for church service. But for all of them God's presence is manifested both in the social motivation of love (Spirit) and in the intelligible particularity and concreteness of grace (word).

The Role of the Spirit

We speak of the *Holy Spirit* as the divine power which comes from God to enable us to know and serve God and the neighbor from within ourselves. It is a way of speaking of God as a presence close at hand, entering into our subjectivity and doing good through us, giving us the ability to sustain confidence and joy. The Holy Spirit is God at work wherever there is love and mercy, gathering such actions out of the relativity and arbitrariness of the individual and into a universal, spiritual movement for human dignity.

The Holy Spirit is behind justice, loving-kindness, and self-sacrifice wherever they are found, making them into objective values that do not depend on diverse and inconsistent individuals. One is "possessed" by the Spirit that works its righteous love in the world. The Spirit corresponds to our capacity for growth and discernment and to the much neglected process of "sanctification" in western religious culture.

The Role of the Word

We speak of the *word* as God's work on our understanding, pointing to the concreteness by which God unconditionally affirms human life, with all its alienation and suffering, in the cross of Christ. It is also another way of speaking of God—as the One made known to us in Christ. It speaks of the covenant relation by which God, the Creator and Judge (Destroyer) of the world, is at the same time its Redeemer and Savior.

The Word and the Spirit

The need to ponder these distinctions is related both to the task of preaching and to the many other ministries of the church, including the ministry of the laity. The word and the Spirit underlie all ministry of God's people. That is why sound preaching is indispensable. But in certain traditions the tendency has been to emphasize one or the other, thus obscuring either the dynamic of the Spirit or the clarity of the Word.

Much of contemporary church life has neither spiritual vitality nor theological expression. The vocabulary and interpretation of the Christian faith have been left to Fundamentalists and Pentecostal sectarians. The Spirit and the word are part of all true ministry in Christ's name, for a living faith is both active in reconciling love and grounded in redeeming grace. Without a theology of the word, we tend to replace the person of Christ and the practical implications of "atonement" with secular versions of middle-class idealism or general religiosity. We miss the central point of Christianity: the material relevance of Jesus and of membership in his company of disciples. The struggle for life and for a just balance in the world no longer touches us directly or enlists our total support.

All ministries of the church are sustained both by the Spirit and by the word of God. The preacher is not the only minister for us to appreciate or to be concerned about. Other forms of ministry even seem better adapted to the needs of American society, and this is why we raise the question about preaching as mission. The preacher must be aware of her or his role—precisely because he or she is responsible for serving the word of God, on which all other ministries depend. The word of God exists apart from preaching, but preaching specifically relates the word to all Christian ministry.

The Uniqueness of the Bible

It is obvious from the above that the "word of God" does not mean the Bible but a manner of God's self-revealing activity and presence. The word of God is God's own dealing with the world. However, the definite concreteness of the word of God necessarily sets the Bible at the center of human experience. At the same time, it makes clear what the Bible is—not a separate history in competition with all other history, but one that is identified in a unique way with the struggles and sufferings of all peoples and cultures. The particularity of grace means the story of God's covenant with Israel and the fulfillment of this covenant in Jesus, the Christ, who died and was raised for all.

For Christians, as for Jews, Muslims, Hindus, Buddhists, and even Communists, the written word is indispensable. Christians have sometimes given the Bible distorted meanings along the lines of other religions and ideologies—as a strict code of ritual conduct, an ageless wisdom, a mythology, a theosophy of secret meanings, or as a triumphalistic manual for violence and war. Through the centuries, the "Christian religion" has suffered every distortion and exaggeration that is potentially alienating in all religions. But the Bible is none of these.

While the other scriptures are also meant to be liberating and ennobling in human life—and so they are among the great spirits, mystics, and humanists—the Bible is different from all of them. It is the long history of a people, told in many ways and from various kinds of sources, in the light of God's coming into the world in a unique way: *as liberation, grace, and courage for a truly human life*.

This is very different from the 5,000 volumes of the teachings of the Buddha, the verbal inspiration to Mohammed as the sole author of the Koran, or the magnificent intrigues of the Ramayana epic. Admittedly, the Bible must be seen in its particularity alongside great stores of ancient literature in North Africa, Pre-Columbian America, China, India, and the rest of Asia, about which we are appallingly ignorant in the West. But the many books of the Bible, each of them historically conditioned and dealing with truth for specific situations, embody the wholly original narration of the "philanthropy" of God. This is the truth and hope implied in all religions. Only in the Bible is God depicted as forgiving love for the human creation, not as an idea or intuition or primal force inherent within human experience, but as revelation and intervention that confront this world in its injustice and absolutism. God reaches out to turn us around and to save us from inhumanity and the rule of death.

The Bible Defines Humanity

But what is truly human? Is not any human experience "truly human"? Are not cruelty and torture and bloodthirstiness just as truly human as care, compassion and gentleness? Are not power, self-satisfaction, wealth, and complacency truly human, since all of us have hidden yearnings for these things? Is anything more truly human than death?

The Bible defines what it means to be truly human. The intervention of the divine word and Spirit in human experience and history establishes humanity as *existence before God*. Whatever is arbitrary and exploitive in human relations is sin; it is obedience to demonic powers, discouragement in the face of mortality, a form of idolatry. Sin is rebellion against God and against humanity. The incarnation of word and Spirit results in the overcoming of sin by grace and makes possible conditional but real justice and love in the world. True humanity is reconcilation and obedience, the world liberated from the power of sin and death through Jesus Christ. It is the blessing of God for the whole of creation.

True humanity is Jesus of Nazareth. That is what "Christ" means today. The Bible centers true humanity in the expectation of the kingdom of God, conditionally present in the structures of a just community and unconditionally present in the awaited Messiah.

Failing to love God and one's neighbor is correctly called inhuman and dehumanizing, a sin against one's own humanity and a rejection of the divine blessing. This corruption of the human spirit is not due only to our inability to achieve moral perfection because of our finitude; it is a result of our rejecting, suppressing, and ignoring grace. True humanity is a quality of life that is well-pleasing (*eudokias*) to God. It is ultimately embodied in Jesus of Nazareth as he was obedient unto death on the cross, but it is also found in responsive persons of all nations and cultures by the power of God's good creation and the generosity of the human spirit. The truly human is the reflected image of God (*imago dei*) in all persons, not without their contradictions but without radical alienation, finite but "well-pleasing" to God (Luke 2:14).

The Bible and Preaching

So the Bible has special significance for preaching. The word of God comes through the Bible, even if it is not identified with the Bible exclusively or at every point. The Bible is necessary in preaching because it narrates a history in which God is uniquely present, not a religious philosophy about God nor a spiritual experience that intimates God. The events that occur in the history of its people are, of course, interpreted by faith, but the identity of this people and their struggle for continuity are objectively determined only by the true God of righteous love. God is with them, and this is what makes them who they are. In turn, the world learns through this people who God is and that God both judges and redeems the world in fulfillment of the covenant, expressed universally in the story of Noah and concretely in the faith of Moses. All nations are blessed in the seed of Abraham and Sarah. They all look to the one Creator and Redeemer, who is present and active in their own special histories and cultures.

In this sense, "salvation" really is from the Jews, as Jesus said to the woman of Samaria (John 4:22). The tree of Jesse is no abstraction, and the truth of Jesus is not verbal memorization, but a quality of life. The church we serve and the gospel we preach have living roots in biblical soil. For this reason we need a deeper fellowship and more frequent sharing with Jews. This will help us to know the Bible as they know it, as well as to overcome anti-Semitism toward both Jews and Arabs. It will keep us from the temptation to spiritualize and to privatize the Bible.

The Bible is necessary for the communication of the word of God because it enables each preacher to put his or her calling within the framework of actual events. It is the Bible, not the originality or spiritual gifts of the preacher, that projects the authentic nature of God's relation to persons through faith. For this reason the preacher is not dependent on his or her subjectivity. The preacher simply serves to mediate a reality that has its own power and appeal within the consciousness of those who hear.

A Third World Viewpoint

Sometimes the question of the function of preaching becomes very significant in people's lives. A few years ago the National Council of Churches in the Philippines, under martial law and divided in political opinion, with many of its leaders arrested and tortured, produced the following *Statement on the Use of the Pulpit*.[4] It is a reminder to us that preachers have a responsibility to speak a certain kind of word and that the church needs to have the word spoken in the midst of the world's problems. The statement can help us to see the true calling of the pulpit, which God in coming generations may will to make as strong as, or stronger than, it has ever been in the past:

> *The sermon is normally the form in which the Word of God is interpreted from the pulpit in the midst of a worshiping congregation.* The sermon is a particular form of address spoken to a congregation at worship. It aims to preach the Word of God in all of its dimensions. To do that it must be based on Holy Scriptures. It must interpret Holy Scriptures properly; it must expound the meaning of a text then and now clearly and specifically. To interpret the Word of God in a sermon means making the Word of God *bear upon* a specific problem, a particular situation, a concrete issue, a definite life situation. The Word of God is nothing unless it strikes people in their lives, their communities, institutions, cultures, and their destinies. And it strikes them in judgment, mercy, and promise, aiming at *change* (repentance) to bring about more love, more justice, more truth, more freedom, more peace, and more praises of God in human life and affairs.
>
> If, therefore, the Word of God is properly interpreted in a sermon, a preacher may have to draw out specific implications and conclusions that indicate the significance of God's Word for now, for today, in our contemporary life situation. And the implication or conclusion should be critical of current trends, prevailing situations, etc.
>
> But whether critical or not, the meaning of the Word of God must be shown as indeed the Word of God, based on Scriptures properly interpreted, and not the meaning of some other philosophy or ideology or religious commitment! Whenever contemporary realities are commented upon from the pulpit, whether critically or not, and the comment is not seen to derive

directly from a proper interpretation of Scripture, but comes from an assumed philosophy or ideology held on grounds other than the Word of God, then the pulpit is abused.

3

Jesus and Liberation Preaching

The center of our faith is Jesus Christ and him crucified. We rise at the reading of the Gospel, not other portions of the Bible, because Jesus is there and speaks there. It is appropriate that we ask: What was Jesus' attitude toward "liberation"?

The Gospels tell of Roman occupation of Jesus' country and of expectations that a Messiah would come to set the people free. A resistance group called the Zealots were active in Jesus' time. They continued their struggle until Rome took action that resulted in total repression under Vespasian and his son Titus in A.D. 70. The famed fortress of Masada, on the shores of the Dead Sea, held out until A.D. 74, when 900 Jews died there, the last by their own hand. Clearly, the struggle for liberation was a part of the world of Jesus.

Luke places Jesus' birth at the time of a census by Quirinius, governor of Syria, for purposes of taxation. Once the enemies of Jesus tried to trap him with a question: Should a Jew pay taxes to Caesar? It is significant that he refused to side either with the Zealots, who opposed paying taxes, or with the

Sadducees, who favored it. Jesus implied that there was a third way.

Whether we regard Jesus as a revolutionary or not, his life and message are linked to that elusive but fruitful concept of *another way*. We may read an analysis of the political setting of Jesus' ministry in S. G. F. Brandon's *Jesus and the Zealots*. Oscar Cullman presents an opposing view in *Jesus and the Revolutionaries*. John Howard Yoder has a stimulating pacifist interpretation in *The Politics of Jesus*. All of these writers agree that Jesus belonged to an historical context and made decisions within it, in accord with his understanding of Judaism and of God's will and covenant. Our reading and interpretation of scripture must take this very seriously. To interpret Jesus apart from the Old Testament, to which he was intimately related, leads us to see him as "personal Savior," with no real interest in changing the world. Careful attention to his use of the Old Testament yields a different conclusion.

Jesus and the Prophets of Justice

Jesus was selective in his use of Jewish history and religion. In his sermon at Nazareth, in which he set forth the purposes of his work, he cited Isaiah 61, a part of the theology of resistance and hope of deliverance that was produced during the Babylonian exile (Luke 4:14-21). He also used this text in response to a question about his work from the disciples of John the Baptist (Matthew 11:2-6). Out of all the traditions of his people, Jesus came down on the side of the prophets of justice with their hope for the kingdom of God. Note that many of these prophets were also priests! There is no real conflict between the service of God as worship and the service of God as love and justice.

In the same sermon, Jesus cited Isaiah 58:6. In 1953, James Muilenberg wrote that all the verbs in this verse "express the idea of liberation."[5]

That was long before anyone talked of a theology of liberation! Deliverance is the true theme of biblical faith. Jesus defined himself largely in relation to the latter chapters of

Isaiah, with their message of universalism through the presence and righteous love of God, redemption of the poor and the oppressed, the figure of the suffering servant of the Lord, and the coming of God's kingdom.

The church has for the most part echoed the message of liberation which Jesus derived from Isaiah. But many Christians have not, and this is why there are differences among us today. There are many today like Louis XIV, who saw no conflict between attending mass in the royal chapel every day while his troops harrassed and murdered the families of Protestants in a betrayal of justice and fraternity.

Jesus was executed as a rebel between two "guerilla fighters." They were bandits who represented the protest against Roman rule. With the help of a small group of Sadducees and Pharisees, the Romans put Jesus to death. As early as Mark 3:6, we read that the Pharisees "held counsel with the Herodians against him, how to destroy him." What resulted was seen by the early church as a fulfillment of Isaiah 53: "Surely he has borne our griefs. . . . By oppression and judgment he was taken away."

Jesus chose where he would stand within this Jewish tradition, or perhaps we should say that *God chose him*. Jesus stood with the unknown prophet whom scholars have come to call Second Isaiah. This man stood at a critical turning point in Jewish history. How did he become the prophet of liberation, of hope in the future, and of good news for the poor? Traditional readings of scripture fail to understand this because we fail to see the historical background, because we read from the standpoint of the saved rather than the lost, the learned rather than the masses, the rich rather than the poor. What is the setting of Second Isaiah that determined his theology? His themes are Jerusalem, the covenant with Abraham, creation, forgiveness, salvation, the action of the Holy Spirit, the importance of the Exodus, liberation from oppression, the sending of the righteous king, and God's justice (Isaiah 48:21; 51:9f-10; 55:3; 58:6-9). Second Isaiah, like Jesus, used a selective approach toward the rich traditions of his people.

Jesus and Josiah's Reform

A second portion of scripture that greatly influenced Jesus was that related to the reforms of King Josiah in 621 B.C. Here was another radical turning point in Israel's history and theology. A book of law was "found" in the temple, perhaps placed there in the hope that it might be discovered and heeded. It was probably compiled by temple priests from earlier material available to them.

The book, now a part of what we call Deuteronomy, called the people of Judah to a renewed understanding of their relationship to God. The king received the book, read it, and ordered its principles and commands into effect. This was the real beginning of Judaism, preparing the people to endure the exile in Babylon which began in 597 B.C. It helped them to remain faithful even though Jerusalem and its temple were destroyed in 586 B.C. They developed the synagogue and the rabbinate to replace temple and priesthood. They realized that God is everywhere, not just on the temple mount. They began to compile and preserve the holy writings that told of Adam and Eve, Cain and Abel, Noah, Abraham and Sarah, Jacob and his wives and children—all the people who prepared the way for Moses, who marks the real historical beginning of Israel as God's people.

At this time of turmoil in western Asia, God was reorganizing history! Josiah reigned during a time when the old Assyrian empire was breaking up and when new, gigantic political forces were beginning to arise. One of these was Egypt, and another was Babylon. Many small kingdoms between these great powers became political pawns. It was time for the kingdom of Judah to become vitally aware of its own national destiny (2 Kings 22—23).

In Judah, including Jerusalem itself, we find all the evil practices of other religions, tending to undermine faithfulness to the God who brought the Hebrews out of bondage in Egypt. We find worship of idols, orgiastic participation in fertility cults, use of phallic symbols, and religious prostitution. The mighty pagan gods such as Moloch, the sun, the moon, and the stars were worshiped. We find astrology, talking with the spirits of the dead, magic, fortune telling, witchcraft, and a quest for good luck by gambling. The religious symbolism touched people at the point of their deepest fears and longings. We even hear of human sacrifice!

Josiah tried to change all this. He recognized that Judah had become a religious melting pot in which the very identity of his people might soon be lost. Their self-understanding was bound up with the Lord God, who had rescued them from slavery in Egypt. What Josiah did preserved this people. Unlike all the other tribes and peoples of that period, they were not assimilated or lost to history. They remained a sign of God's dealing with the world. Josiah and the reforming priests and prophets realized that the people's identity was linked to their delivery by God from the land of Egypt.

Thus the passover, the sabbath, circumcision, and other signs of obedience to God were rediscovered or interpreted anew. The people were reminded about the nature of humanity, human destiny, the mystery of sin, and the hope of God's grace. A line was created that would lead directly to Jesus, and from him to us. Here began a religion based in history (what happens) rather than in imagination or in romantic idealism. It is concerned with what matters for human relationships, with the suffering and death of human persons. This religion is concerned not with what we believe about the supernatural or about our own mysterious origins and composition, but with how we live before the God who loves every creature.

Jesus and Old Testament Law

Laws believed to have been given by God to Moses were "rediscovered" as the written traditions of Judaism took form. They told how the nation was to be governed, how God was to be worshiped, and how persons were to relate to one another. The people were to be holy as God is holy. Many of these laws are found in Exodus 21—23 and in Deuteronomy 12—26. Deuteronomy 29:1-19 has been called the "Apostle's Creed of the Old Testament" because it sums up the new demand for obedience to God based on God's gracious act in Israel's history.

Here was the turning point which led to the development of Judaism as a world religion, to Jesus the prophet of Nazareth, and to the Christian church. It was the creation of a *people*, not a nation. This tended to be forgotten when, at the time of Constantine, Christianity became the state religion. The authentic faith had its origin among an oppressed people whom God liberated from Egypt and then commanded to be merciful toward the unprotected, the widow, and the orphan. Human exploitation was seen as rejection of the covenant with God. It was denial of God's rule and kingdom.

Concern for the oppressed and the suffering lay at the base of Jewish laws and institutions. Much of the law has to do with daily life and the regulation of society. We see reflections of the ancient Code of Hammurabi, of Canaanite civilization, and of the peoples with whom Israel had contact and conflict through many centuries.

The single line which tied these laws to God was the people's memory of slavery in Egypt and their lack of worth in the eyes of the world. Their institutions testified not just to a concept or a religious ethic but to the righteousness of God, including both divine love and divine wrath. This had implications primarily for the people of ancient Judah, but it came to apply to all human beings. It was an affirmation of the worth of every human person. Again and again these people were drawn to God by an awareness of God' grace, requiring justice on their part.

This was not a justice rooted in the wisdom of a king or in the insights of philosophers and lawgivers. It was rooted in God's love and will for the world. The stranger, the widow, and the orphan represent the oppressed—what Israel would always have been without God's grace. Israel must seek conditions which affirm, protect, and elevate the humanity of the oppressed. God is their advocate, and to neglect them is to make an enemy of God. Many centuries later, when the great prophet Jesus appeared, he found within the body of Jewish law what expressed its historical genius—the law of love.

Jesus expressed the basic Jewish law when he taught the world the love of neighbor. *The one motive for every act is the fact that God loves us.* God shows love toward us in leading the people out of bondage in Egypt and in sending Christ to die for our sins. We acknowledge and respond to this love in the way we treat one another. The religious heritage of the church has nothing to do with casting out demons, speaking to the dead, interpreting the stars, or foreseeing the future. It has to do with liberation of persons by justice and love in their social context. This is the key to the health and wellbeing of the church and of our culture. Even our prayer, worship, and communion are derived from the God who loves the world and who suffers with people (1 Corinthians 11:23-26). The covenant of just institutions produces a new covenant of community and a dawning of God's liberating and saving grace for the world.

The Hope Jesus Offers

Josiah's reform in 621 B.C. and the work of prophets like Jeremiah pointed forward to God's definitive act of liberation through the coming of the Messiah. To some, this meant a political leader like David; to others, it meant the suffering servant of God. The temptations of Jesus after his baptism clearly show his rejection of the political role. As revolutionary as Jesus was, he was not a Zealot. We must be aware of the extent to which all of his life work and teaching were shaped by the growing resistance to Rome, constantly increasing repression, and finally open revolution leading to the destruction of Jerusalem by Titus in A.D. 70. It is significant that Jesus offered a different way to deal with oppression. The Jewish church or church of Jerusalem, about which we know almost nothing because of the destruction of the city, apparently continued to think of him as a national Messiah. It was Paul and the Gentile church that spread across the Roman world and proclaimed Jesus as the universal Savior and Redeemer.

Jesus of Nazareth cannot be separated from the long, agonizing and humanizing history of his people. He selected his theological understanding from this tradition. In all his teaching he remained true to the covenant, a commitment to love and justice in society because of the love of God in liberating Israel from Egypt. He fulfilled in himself the hope of a new covenant.

It is not possible, as the reformers of Josiah's time believed, to read history in terms of the unfailing victory of justice, humanity, and truth. Josiah himself was killed by Pharaoh Neco at Megiddo in 609 B.C. Jeremiah was taken unwillingly by refugees to Egypt, where he disappeared from history. Jerusalem was sacked twice and the people deported. The tragedy and irony of life found no satisfactory answer in the law or in the struggle for justice. Nor was there any way to make up for people's failure to keep the law. People of faith, like Jeremiah, looked beyond these inadequacies:

> Behold, the days are coming, says the Lord, when I will make a new covenant with the house of Israel and the house of Judah, not like the covenant that I made with their fathers when I took them by the hand to bring them out of the land of Egypt, my covenant which they broke, though I was their husband, says the Lord. But this is the covenant which I will make with the house of Israel after those days, says the Lord: I will put my law within them, and I will write it upon their hearts; and I will be their God, and they shall be my people. And no longer shall each man teach his neighbor, and each his brother, saying, "Know the Lord," for they shall all know me, from the least of them to the greatest, says the Lord; for I will forgive their iniquity, and I will remember their sin no more (Jeremiah 31:31-34).

An echo of this scripture is found in the writings of Paul:

> For I received from the Lord what I also delivered

to you, that the Lord Jesus on the night when he was betrayed took bread, and when he had given thanks, he broke it, and said, "This is my body which is for you. Do this in remembrance of me." In the same way also the cup, after supper, saying, "This cup is the new covenant in my blood. Do this, as often as you drink it, in remembrance of me." For as often as you eat this bread and drink the cup, you proclaim the Lord's death until he comes (1 Cor. 11:23-26).

The Jewish covenant of just institutions produced the covenant of a new humanity and a new community in Christ. It was a new dawning of God's liberating and saving grace for the world.

Like the historical concreteness of the Exodus, of Josiah's reform, of Israel's laws and Israel's suffering, the cross of Christ is an historical reality that gives definiteness to the faith and mission of the church. Jesus himself reached back into the concrete experiences and the relevant institutions of his people to find and hold up love as the central commandment. Humanization and liberation are central in the Bible. It is God's greatest blessing. We see this in Leviticus 19:17f.:

> You shall not hate your brother in your heart, but you shall reason with your neighbor, lest you bear sin because of him. You shall not take vengeance or bear any grudge against the sons of your own people, but *you shall love your neighbor as yourself*; I am the Lord.

And further on in this chapter:

> When a stranger sojourns with you in your land, you shall not do him wrong. The stranger who sojourns with you shall be to you as the native among you, and you shall love him as yourself; for you were strangers in the land of Egypt: I am the Lord your God (Leviticus 19:33f).

In his own person, Jesus brings the forgiveness that enables us to start anew. The Holy Spirit works within us to implement love and justice. In the concrete historical experience of Jews and Christians, justice is not a way to interpret in a social context the "ideal" of love. Christianity and Judaism are not idealistic. They do not begin with our ideas, our inspiration, or our feelings. Rather, they call for actions of love toward people as they are and where they are. Such love grows out of the liberating laws and humanizing institutions of a people who seek to do right before God. Such love brings the transformation of people's hearts through forgiveness and reconciliation.

Jesus found and incarnated the basic Jewish law. This is why the religious heritage of the church has nothing to do with a fatalistic theology of God's omnipotence. It has to do with the liberating of persons through justice and love, their survival under hellish conditions through remembrance of the cross, and the unshakable conviction through the Holy Spirit that life and right are worthwhile.

This is the key to the health and wellbeing of our church and of our culture, rooted in the theology of Jesus. It is nourished and incorporated into our lives by prayer, worship, and communion with him who is love for the world. Such health and wellbeing are the creation of a community whose sole purpose is to raise the level of life and the hope of people. If it is not doing this, it is not any good any more. To the extent that the community does this, it is the fulfillment through the power of Jesus Christ of God's covenant and blessing given to Abraham:

> I will make of you a great nation, and I will bless you, and make your name great, so that you will be a blessing. I will bless those who bless you, and him who curses you I will curse; and by you all the families of the earth shall bless themselves (Genesis 12:2f).

All our material hopes, all our longing for a legitimate prosperity, happiness, and peace are there summed up!

4

Liberation Preaching for Conversion

The twentieth century has witnessed an unprecedented effort to achieve Christian unity. The Bible has played a significant part in this. It asserts the foundation on which the church stands. It testifies to the power of God, which calls a people into being for the sake of the whole world. Unity is an expression of God's mission and purpose for the church, which is a sign of the unity of all peoples for the sake of life itself. The Bible makes clear that God in Christ gives unity to the church in the very mission given to the church.

The problem in the American church is not primarily one of unity. It is ideological complacency and a lack of a sense of God's mission. Personal anxiety and a nameless dread lead many to seek the sense of security offered by closely-knit groups, congregational and denominational. But members of such groups often forget that the group itself has a calling from God. Such a calling is directed to the body as a whole and is not just the sum of its parts or a projection of the individual preferences and opinions of its members. We must do more than take a vote to decide what the church should be doing. Christ must be the center of the church's life, and the church's will must correspond to his will. The low priority given to Christian unity in congregations is merely a symptom of something more serious—a lack of awareness of the gospel itself.

Cultivation of the Spirit

The written word of God must not be too lightly dismissed; we should read it more than we do! It is a guide for meditation and for a deeper knowledge of Jesus Christ. Buddhism and other world religions remind us of the impoverishment of our lives in modern society and of the need to go aside for contemplation. Reflection on the prophets and the New Testament, and prayer based on the Psalms, draw us closer to the presence of God in the contradictions of daily life.

Many of our social and personal problems come from the inability to find time to center upon ourselves and our mental and physical resources. The body is an organism that needs to be understood, and our emotions affect us both physically and mentally. Jogging is popular not just because it helps us physically, but also because it makes us feel better about our lives and our work. Most of us know the thrill of participation in sports. Young people today speak of "getting our act together." In our rush-and-tumble existence, we need to be more unified, more centered, and more "mellow."

The church has a mission to help American people find their place as individuals within the universe. One important way is to encourage meditation, worship, and the reading and understanding of the Scriptures.

The trinitarian content and order of the liturgy are more important for our inner life than they appear at first glance. Of course, there is a danger of lifeless repetition of words and acts. But there is a reason for the classical formulation of Christian worship: our expression of wonder, the law of God to love one another, the confession of sin, the words of grace from the Bible, the assurance of pardon from the minister, thanksgiving, and intercession.

There is movement in this liturgy that is definite and effective. If it is made meaningful and if it comes from the heart, participants go out from this service with a sense that something has occurred. God has really done something, and life has changed. The sinner is accepted and loved. He or she tastes the freedom from sin that is more powerful than our own will, a power that enables us to turn around and walk in a new way (repentance).

Even the forgiven sinner is still a sinner, and the victory over sin is made complete in the love and suffering of Christ, not so much as we would wish in the framework of our daily lives. To think otherwise would be the greatest illusion and perfectionism. But the experience of forgiveness is at the very heart of the Christian faith, and the liturgy expresses that forgiveness as the word of God. That doesn't mean that it has to be ritualistic or formal. It happens as a direct act of God. It happens now. It happens definitely. The sense of cleansing is a kind of exorcism that worship needs to recover. The Southeast Asia Institute for Liturgy and Music described it thus:

> Through its liturgy the church constantly recalls its faith and hope in the Word of God, is united and strengthened by the Holy Spirit, participates in the saving acts of Christ and is made one with him and his loving purpose of redemption.[6]

Many ministers have forgotten to make the pastoral prayer a summary of this liturgical act. George Buttrick used to say that the ACTS of prayer were adoration, confession, thanksgiving, and supplication. One doesn't often hear this much breadth in today's pastoral prayers.

The singing of responses in worship is particularly meaningful when the congregation responds in a way that is meditative and expressive. Some responses have a Gregorian origin. Some are from the psaltery of the Reformation. Others come from recent hymns and even contemporary songs of the church. We should learn from the Eastern Orthodox churches that the liturgy is as important in the life of Christian people as is the sermon. We need preaching as a base for mission, but it must be a part of vital, doctrinally rich, scripturally founded liturgical creativity.

Preaching on Social Issues

How shall we preach from the Bible in a way that serves the liberating word of God? It is not by looking for the private, emotional, or sentimental clue to God's love for the individual. Neither is it to turn away from the basic issues of American life: racism, sexism, crime in the streets, crime in corporate boards and in unions, nuclear militarism, and hatred in the form of incipient fascism, the enemy of every liberal democracy.

No! Preaching must address the real evils of our time. Mammon and the cohorts of death are still around and within us, almost as literally as they are in literature like *Faust* and in movies like *The Verdict*. Restraints on the forces of evil through the power of law and the balance of justice are needed, and biblical preaching will make this clear.

Biblical preaching must deal with ethics. There is no such thing as "Christian ethics"; there is only human ethics. There are, however, ethical implications of the Christian faith. To discern these we need theological reflection on human conduct through preaching the word of God. Christian faith is just one form of religion, and its ethical content shows what kind of religion it is.

However, social issues, as well as matters of personal growth and devotion, are *objects of* preaching, not its subject. The subject is the gospel! The work of the gospel is full community and justice before God. It is mercy and love in all of the concrete circumstances of life, not abstraction or wishful thinking. Social problems, economic and political acts that deny human dignity, are to be included in preaching; but they are not themes for moralistic lectures that draw on the secular expertise of the preacher. He or she ought to know something about interpersonal relations, sociology, and international affairs. But the subject for which preaching is uniquely responsible is God's business with the world, reflected in the concrete reality of the Bible and brought to bear on the concrete reality of the hearers. The light is the gospel, not the preacher, but the preacher uses that light to probe and change the dark corners of human existence.

What, then, is the possibility of pastors and their coworkers consistently finding in the Scriptures the message appropriate for Christian sermons? This question needs more than one simple answer. It involves groups working on the lectionary together with the minister. Prayer and the Spirit bring unexpected fruits. The holiness of God is seen in the freedom and unsuspected versatility of any creative endeavor. Ministers and congregations may find many ways to embody the gospel ecumenically in mission.

Looking for the Gospel in the Text

One way to discover the gospel was suggested by a French pastor, André de Robert, founder of the community of Villeméterie: "Study the text in its context and ask, 'Where is the good news of Jesus Christ here?'" One looks for grace. The signs are there. The preacher's task is to discern the good news in the heart of the text and to proclaim it. When she or he finds it, it becomes the key to a sermon. The preacher can say, "This is why I am preaching from this text today."

We begin our Bible study *inductively*, letting the text take us where it will. It has to seize our imagination and to come alive for us. By the power of association and contrast or similarity, it embraces our lives and situations today. Every sermon begins as a Bible study in order to recognize grace and to proclaim it in our immediate circumstances. We never begin with assumptions about creation or about God's plan. We begin with the stories of the Bible, and we see what they have come to mean to suffering humanity over twenty centuries.

One looks for the way in which the grace of God in Jesus, understood as the Jewish Messiah, liberates men and women within the conditional framework of their particular history.

We see how God's grace enables them to participate in changing the direction and the effect of their history. Instead of submitting to "powers and principalities," either as victims or as accomplices, the people whom God activates with the divine word and deed become personalities. They act out of hope. They are made truly human and personal, bearing the marks of freedom.

In the text before us, the eschatological Kingdom is manifested in some way through them for liberation and blessing. The Kingdom is not a Utopian dream, but an ecstatic perception and work of the Spirit. In the text is joy and love, motivated by the divine Presence. Such inductive study and preaching is not merely analytical. It is devotional in the sense that it enhances worship as well as reflection. But the grace can be found in the text and then given to others!

In the presence of Jesus, people remember the promise and deliverance of the past. They embody the hope of the future as a concrete alternative in their current existence. They become people of the Spirit, not withdrawing from the struggle and the risk of their liberation in a substitute and compensatory world of feeling and imagination, but finding God present in their real situation. God makes their seemingly isolated cases of suffering into a part of divine love and care for people and for the whole creation, part of a new awareness of humanity and of "inalienable human rights" as the essential structure of history and being. Against all appearances, whether they be worldly powers or psychological dread, the human spirit knows that it belongs to God eternally in the forgiveness and peace of God's righteous love. This love is relentless in its punishment of every oppression and is merciful to sustain the faithful in every adversity.

"Where is the good news in this text?" The question represents an openness to what the Scriptures have to say, not in a theological consistency throughout the Bible, but in a coherence given by Jesus himself. This coherence is deliberately selective. It extends backward through the Old Testament in Jesus' recognition of prophetic realism as authentic response to

God. It is evident in Jesus' association of suffering with the expectation of God's anointed Savior—the suffering servant rather than King David, a new Zion rather than a holy war. This coherence extends laterally through the Gospels in Jesus' relation to outcasts, publicans and sinners, and in his preaching of the joy and assurance of the kingdom of God at hand. This coherence extends forward through the Acts, the Epistles, and the Apocalypse, which show the effect Jesus had on his world, the universality given by faith to his redemptive death on the cross, and the community of love and sharing that represented the new life of participation in his resurrection.

The Scriptures everywhere contain this good news, either through the historical continuity to which the story of Christ belongs, or by contrast to that continuity. The story of Christ is found in the way the Bible was put together, in the captivity and the formative experience of Judaism in Babylon, and in the early liturgy of the creation narratives. The story of Christ is in the Passover, celebrating the central event that constituted the people through their liberation from slavery in Egypt. The story of Christ is in the prophets, the priests, the kings, the Sabbath, the Psalms, the covenants, and the Wisdom Literature.

The story of Christ is in the opinions and biases as well as the theological profundity of St. Paul. It is in the political denunciation of Rome and the religious vision of the Apocalypse, which echoes Isaiah and the lamb of God who takes away the world's sin. The good news is sometimes directly, sometimes indirectly and obliquely present in the biblical text, either by affiliation or denial. The historical person Jesus Christ is the key to authentic revelation in the Bible. Liberation for the glory of God, and grace given to those who have faith, are clues to the presence of the good news at every point.

Scripture provides the narrative in which God's sovereign action with the creation takes place concretely and definitively in Jesus. He corresponds to that aspect of the Jewish messianic expectation that renounces every use of manipulative power, human or divine, to overcome the human or demonic enemies of God. The resurrection does not point to the victory of "life" over death, but to the victory of *God* over death and to our true life in God through joy and obedience in the world and hope in the Kingdom to come.

The preacher tells the story of God's love in a way that does not spiritualize it away from the struggles and constraints of power, and does not sentimentalize its ascendancy over the uncertainties of self-awareness. The sermon is not a discourse about God, but an attempt to narrate what God has done to save the world. God is known in and through the Bible, and where the good news is found there, we also find implications for the experiences that persons undergo today.

This becomes meaningful for hearers in the congregation through the suggestiveness of grace in their own minds and through the seeking of God's will in their own personal and social activities. The good news is that, in the incalculable chances and complexities of life, where experience shows that no persons can justify themselves and where all are sinners before God, where all people and all works pass away like the leaves of summer, where all are sinned against by every abuse of power, nevertheless God has justified the world in Jesus Christ, in his suffering and his future.

The preacher seeks to be used to awaken and nourish faith. The only way to do this is through telling the scripture story and through the global ministry of the church—lay, local, and worldwide. Example is convincing: practice that gives rise to beautiful ideas, not beautiful ideas in themselves. The congregation must see very clearly what it actually *does* and what the God of the Scriptures would have it to *do*.

The Process of Conversion

The role of scripture is to convert hearts to the love of God. This is a constant process in the church, for there are always changes in people's lives that qualify or even corrupt their original commitment. Like everything that is alive and is undergoing activity and change, conversion is a process. Conversion is always a discovery or rediscovery of spiritual freedom, of personal worth, and of joy in God's forgiveness and universal love.

The preacher must see in scripture a description of men and women today whose hearts are hardened against God or whose sufferings evoke the memory of Calvary. Attitudes toward South Africa or Nicaragua are a case in point. The church of the New Testament embodies a new life in Christ. It tells of the gift of the Spirit that contrasts with the understanding of many of today's Christians. The role of scripture is not to lead to "enlightenment" or to a private religious experience. Its role is to turn us around, to convert us from obedience to false gods, from destructive purposes, from impulses of resentment and revenge. It converts us to respect for a higher justice than our own and to the pursuit of simplicity, humanism, and peace.

Such conversion is not impossible in middle-class America. Its preparation is already present, if not in the exploiters of land and the ravishers of Black, Hispanic, Asian, Native American, and poor white communites, then in the struggle and sufferings of the victims, in their faith, and in the bad conscience and the solidarity with them of many others.

Conversion to the compassion of God, the psychological and emotional acceptance of a transcendent grace that turns things around in a surprising way, is not the invention of cultural anthropology or of philosophy of religion. The world of scripture makes its own contribution along with the world of speculation and science. This conversion is the peculiar gift of the Bible, and therefore the Bible is essential to preaching.

Conversion is a process, but it is not a neurosis. It is not something that always eludes our grasp because we can never be sure enough of our state of mind or resolute enough in our commitment. Conversion is first of all a decision about where one wants to walk and dares to stand. It is a simple yes to God. But since Christians have only one locus for the meaning of God, since we only know God in terms of the gospel, conversion is more specifically yes to Jesus as Lord and Savior of the world.

Conversion is a process, but it is first of all something concrete. It is a decisive, irrevocable step, but it is capable of becoming insincere, corrupted, and void. Apostasy is not the same as unbelief. The apostate Christian is one who no longer cares, one who turns his or her back on suffering and the demands of justice. Conversion is acceptance of God's grace and the will to live by divine love. It is faith—a covenant of friendship offered by God and accepted by us. The *devotio moderna* of the late Middle Ages, forerunner of the Reformation, and including John Tauler and Meister Eckhart, represented a society called "The Friends of God." The world could use such friends across all lands and cultures today!

There are not two kinds of Christians: born again and others. Every person is born again when he or she affirms faith and acknowledges God's grace in the rite of baptism. Saying yes to Jesus Christ is not a sectarian ritual but entry into discipleship. The goal of preaching is not to proselytize the world in order to increase the numbers and strength of some denomination. Yes to Christ is an affirmation of one's personal relation to the God revealed by Jesus and acceptance of life in terms of the coming Kingdom.

In the crisis of Jewish history, Jesus made the world aware of itself in a special way, based on God's mercy for all people, especially for the poor. The cross of Jesus liberated the pagan world for true humanity and for progressive, though ambiguous, historical relations. Yes to Christ still means a preference for him, a love for his humanness, and a reflection within one's spirit of *Christ's* Spirit, which continues to live and to reign over history. Such a yes to Christ means *conversion* in the sense that we become part of his world and of his movement. He does not become simply an acquisition of our wisdom or of our sentimentalism.

Conversion does not mean the emotional riot of revivalism; it means choosing a direction for the future. We enter a new kind of life, a rebirth, of which baptism is the symbol. Baptism is not something we think; it is something we *do*. Our being won to the gospel is a concrete event. Baptism is not a cultic ritual of a worn-out and debased Christendom—Protestant, Roman Catholic, or Orthodox—but a sign of the newness of God's kingdom in Christ and the church. It is an act of solidarity with all humanity in the victory of love and justice—the divine *shalom*. We become Christ's disciples, and we live by the life he releases through us.

The world economy is spending 1.3 million dollars per minute for arms. Forty thousand children die daily of hunger and malnutrition. A billion dollars a year is extracted from Zaire, while the people eat less well than ten years ago. Conversion cannot overlook the world's need for a change of ways.

Notes

5

Local Awareness and Global Awareness

The church is not at the service of "internationalism." It invents its own internationalism as it exceeds the limits of every nation and culture. In fact, it breaks their pretenses of absoluteness through its attack upon sin, just as it makes their limitations tolerable through its integration of all peoples in the grace of Christ.

Christian faith is not a sentimental philosophy about "the family of man." Christian faith is a *concrete relation to the whole church through a local congregation*, which is related concretely to other congregations across the world and is in active communication with them through the practical and symbolic nature of their faith and ministry. These relationships are practical in that they involve persons, resources, publications, meetings, and discussions. They are symbolic because they are a sign of the unity of all peoples in their struggle and longing for dignity, peace, and justice.

The gospel and preaching as mission disclose the global solidarity of all human beings in the consciousness of God's love for every particular human being. Global awareness is part of the blessing of Christ. His forgiveness of our sin is the way he deals with our self-enclosure and littleness of spirit, our limited imagination, setting us free to risk attitudes and actions that are favorable to peoples beyond the range of our own race, class, or nation. The love of God and the love of neighbor are "alike" (Matt. 22:37-39) because they are the same love of a center beyond ourselves, for its own sake, not as an obligation, but as an act of freedom. Christ replaces our stony heart with a human heart, and the whole world is not too vast to receive our thanksgiving and our work of love.

Intercession is one of the ways in which the global reality is shown to be present in the spirit of a congregation at worship. Too many prayers are limited to the circle of the congregation: the known sick, people in difficulty, the leaders of the community. This concern is indispensable, but it is also insufficient. To remember those who suffer elsewhere in one's nation as well as abroad is to enter into God's care and love for them. It is a manifestation of the Spirit. It is one way in which people who are oppressed know that they are not alone. It is also a way to motivate action and to stir love to resolution.

God does not depend on our intercessory prayers to be reminded of the world's specific needs and sorrows. But we of the church need to share in the awareness of God's compassion. We ask that God's love be fulfilled in us and in those for whom we pray. We do not ask that God's will be bent to conform to ours, but we ask that God's will may be done, the will that is good for the whole world and that is embodied in the reign of Christ over all unhappiness and evil. The church does not exist for itself alone, either locally or as a world religion. Its intercession is intended to gather together the needs of all human beings and to lift them up in a proclamation of their essential unity and interrelatedness, made known through God's self-revelation through the incarnate Word.

Preaching for Local Awareness

It may seem that preaching global awareness is an extension of preaching about local concerns. The very opposite is the case. Much preaching lacks interest because it does not contain a local relevance that is shaped by worldwide concern. It lacks a sense of mission because it lacks an understanding of mission. Christian practice near at hand is an expression of the unlimited nature of the mission of God. There is an inescapable continuity between "here" and "there." The preacher who is realistic must recognize the global need for signs of hope in order to discern what this means in his or her own community.

No one would argue that local involvement in mission is less important than the world ministries of the church. That would only be an attempt to escape the concreteness in which Christ has set his church. Overseas involvement is not less concrete than local mission, but the effort to separate the two shows misunderstanding of the nature of mission. The concreteness of our world involvement is reflected in the quality and seriousness of our local involvement.

For example, to ignore the evil of racism at home while supporting missionary work in Africa or Latin America is to overlook the struggle against racism in those continents, a struggle that is the principal task of mission there today. Missionaries who return home or church leaders from abroad have been most prophetic in their insights about what the church ought to be doing here about discrimination against minorities, the sufferings of the poor, the needs of the young and the aged, the meaning of Christian presence in the university, and other matters. Such persons have also made us aware of the impact of our elections on the life of people around the world. They have helped in education for world community, in informing people about foreign policy, in showing the need for a simpler and less wasteful lifestyle, and in assessing the quality of life in America.

Thus the local is not less important than the global mission of the church, and the global is not an appendix to the local mission. They are one and the same mission of God. We must think of them as belonging objectively together, not separated by subjective factors. They come together in stewardship when the prevailing international economic order is considered. (It is disorder for many.) And even the local congregation benefits by spending 85 per cent of its income on itself.

Local awareness in preaching means that the preacher is not giving a speech of his or her own choosing, but is proclaiming the word of God for a given situation. Such preaching is not justified by the international impact of local choices, nor by the needs of others, nor by the fact that world ministries need to be sustained in various ways. Rather, such preaching is needed because God's grace thereby becomes known in a liberating and challenging way within the circumstances of a congregation. That is the preacher's joyous task. No salary in some "better job" could ever compensate for this calling to serve the word of God.

The social and cultural forms of the church are necessary and creative, but they are in constant tension with the religious principle itself, which is unavoidably critical, subversive, transforming, and purifying. Otherwise, the church is eventually destroyed in idolatry and ideology. There is always something in the church that is more than the church, and the church knows this, confesses it, and seeks to be faithful to a reality beyond itself. The Spirit, given in the gospel of Christ and the blessing of God, is both against the church and for the church, depending on whether or not the church is an instrument of God for the good of its members and for the blessing of the whole world. Like John the Baptist, the church points to the person of Jesus.

Addressing the Needs of Our Community

Sometimes we do not know what is happening to persons, and we do not know how our local community is organized. We need the sociological realism to look for the causes and sources of power. Most of us don't know the implications of a business going bankrupt or another being organized by various community interests. We do not know how major decisions are made or who the big thieves are. One thing the Marxists have taught us is that the fundamental fact of life is economic, not philosophical. Marx warned of the same dangers that the Bible does: that persons in advantageous positions will see things in terms that are most favorable to the continuation of their privileges. The disadvantaged tend to internalize the reasoning of those they envy, and they rationalize their own disappointments. If they feel superior to some other group, they compensate for their own oppression by oppressing others. Women and children, especially, know how this works.

In its ignorance or blindness toward these circumstances, the church often takes a position that is fruitless from the start. It deals only with personal morality and the spiritual life. Its only social judgment is to be seen in the creation of charitable services, setting a good example by not investing church money in unseemly enterprises, and upholding the values of the surrounding system.

Ultimately, the church does exercise its freedom, for the word of God is not entirely silenced either by the bias of its culture or by the ineffectiveness of the preacher. This is true, at least in part, because the gospel stirs a ready response in the poor, the poor in spirit, and the grandchildren of those who were poor. This is the continuing promise of vitality and liberation within the American democratic process. The gospel will not be made captive, and the general public basically respects the need for church and synagogue to serve the impartial purposes and the judgment of God.

But in spite of that rather eschatological reassurance, the churches are all too often bound to the capitalist system. This does not mean that the churches should favor communism or dream of a social-democrat Utopia. It does mean that the churches should understand critically the system in which they find themselves. This is the "world of the flesh" described in the Bible, so called not because it is sensual and materialist, but because it rejects transcendent judgment and attempts to justify its own power. Churches must be the free space in which basic human concerns are constantly reexamined. Here we can analyze factors that tend to undermine cooperation for human fulfillment and to heighten divisions among the people to their hurt, not only along racial or political lines, but by breaking the solidarity among working people everywhere.

Responding to Social Ills

One problem to which the church should respond is employment. When the churches seek to rally support for farm workers, or seek equal opportunity for minorities and women, or support the organization of non-union workers, they incur the wrath not only of the rich and powerful, but also of workers and citizens whose own interests would be better served by economic justice for all.

How many preachers have examined the effects on a family when someone is enticed to scab for the employer against the majority of the other employees? How many churches support those who fight corrupt unions? Who has sought to comfort the families who lost sons and fathers in Vietnam and to dignify the loss by working for reconciliation with the people of Vietnam—not just the former enemy but also former allies and disillusioned friends? Who has tried to stand against the flood of pornography and drugs, a stream fed by enormous profits? Who has spoken out about pornophonic music encouraged by disk jockeys and television shows? (The point is not that these are objectionable from a puritanical viewpoint, but they flourish because of a way of thinking and doing in affluent societies that undermines the local community itself.)

The church is, above all, a community with a demystifying function in the name of God. Everybody seeks the way, the truth, and the life. If the church can show where these are to be found in order to have a more abundant life, it cannot keep silent. If this means learning from socialism and the many revolutionary societies in the world, so be it. Some of them seem especially successful in eliminating gambling, pimping, begging, organized crime, unemployment, racial discrimination, and disproportionate levels of wealth.

Our reaction to criticism should not be defensiveness, but a recollection of America's democratic traditions and the struggles of our own history in which the gospel has played a large part. What does it mean to love our neighbor in terms of our social institutions? What checks and balances are always necessary in order to limit the effect of self-interest and sin, on the one hand, and to assure freedom on the other?

The sermon is not to portray fantastic solutions, but it must take seriously in the light of God's word both the sinful ambiguities and the hopeful possibilities in the local situation. We do not ask "What would Jesus do?" but "What has God done?" and "What may God be doing in the world now?" What must we do within the options that seem to be open to us and the compromises that must be made? For the rest, we trust God. When we have done all we can and have fought hard for the right, we are still in God's hands. Our greatest test of faith is not to despair when we realize that things are not entirely under our control. But we make no mistake about where our hearts are in the struggle!

Racism is another issue that divides Christians. We never become free of racism. But we can be honest with ourselves, recognize its hold on us, and condemn it in ourselves and in the institutions of society. We can seek accepting relationships, forgiveness, greater understanding, and respect for one another. Because racism is sin, only the cross can remove it. Only the cross touches our tendency to be righteous and good in our own eyes. Only this gift from God can lead us to forgiveness and a new spirit. We do not justify ourselves but must be justified by another!

Training in conflict management can help any congregation. People tend to smooth over differences until it is too late to heal them. Reconciliation does not mean overlooking errors and injustices. It is facing reality with a knowledge that the Christian is not so much *good* as he or she is *loved*. The congregation is not a perfect community, but one that is focused on the cross, from which it derives its strength and direction. The crown of thorns and the empty tomb point both to the real world of human experience and to a transcendent faith. In the person of Jesus, we may see the heartbreak of all humankind as well as the exultation of the human spirit in the offered faith of resurrection.

Dealing with conflict need not be conflict "management" in a manipulative sense. It is being honest, open, respectful, and generous. It means being nonviolent and reasonable, even when pushed beyond the line that we have drawn. Violence is a major problem in North America. But we tend to equate it with change rather than with inertia or resistance to change. Those who protest against the system are seen as violent, while those who maintain it, even at tremendous cost to its victims, see themselves as benign. There is more than one form of violence, and if we are really concerned to root it out, we must deal with our own as well as that of others. The American church needs to exhort the powerful to nonviolence rather than to moralize over the struggles of the poor.

Being the Church in Today's World

Transnational corporations have brought us into a new age of interdependence. They can control the flow of raw materials from one part of the world to another, take advantage of cheap labor wherever they find it, and enjoy tax advantages wherever available. They are responsible to no electorate or government anywhere in the world. The Japanese president of a company moving to the Philippines explained that there was more environmental tolerance in the Philippines than in Japan!

The United States has six per cent of the world's population and uses thirty-five per cent of the annual production from the world's nonrenewable resources. Along with other highly industrialized societies, including both eastern and western Europe, we actually live off the poor countries. It is necessary for Christians to understand this, for it applies directly to the affluent American church. The path of obedience for churches is to protest against unrighteousness, hold out the prospect of God's judgment in grace, and try to turn the resources, power, and influence of the community toward the cause of the oppressed. We must get over the attitude of pity and recognize the global interdependence of a world in which thirty per cent of our own exports are purchased in the Third World and in which we receive vital resources and enormous capital returns from millions living in absolute poverty.

The idea of "foreign missions" no longer applies as it once did. Anything resembling it, including the large number of fundamentalists and independent missionaries abroad, is an affront to the dignity of peoples around the world and to the churches of their own lands. It is often a misguided demonstration of cultural imperialism and of the simplistic view that everyone should believe as we do. In many places, "missionaries" of this kind rival the indigenous church or even seek to steal sheep for their own denomination.

There are few places where American preachers are necessary or even welcome overseas, except as supportive colleagues. There is a continuing need for people who can make a specific contribution and demonstrate the wholeness of the church by linking different cultures. An Argentine pastor explained that the church should make it possible to exchange personnel in order to resist national stereotypes and ideological hatred. Americans should examine their motives. If they are not invited by the indigenous church and its most farsighted leadership, they should stay at home. Partnership in mission, rather than unilateral mission-sending by an agency or congregation, is the only responsible form of missionary work today. Such partnership emphasizes that mission is every bit as important, if not more so, in North America, which needs to hear the Gospel and to recognize the world dimension of our lives.

Far more church members go overseas as tourists, students, business persons, government and military representatives, than will ever be sent again as "missionaries." In fact, these are the "new missionaries" today, if they go from one field of the church's life and witness to another. But even those who travel far are involved in a new way with people on the other side of the globe, and this characterizes the "new world mission" of the church. The gospel speaks to us of the interdependence of each person with and for all other persons. The heart of world mission today is world community, and this heightens rather than diminishes the role of preaching and the impact of the gospel everywhere. The one family of Christ around the world cooperates in prayer, service, and evangelism towards that goal of one humanity that is revealed in the heart of God.

The basic reason for global awareness in the mission of preaching is theological. The glory of God reaches to the far corners of the earth and embraces every people. Likewise, the liberation of Christ as "the Lamb of God that takes away the sins of the world" knows no geographical limits. The very nature of the church points to an international scope.

There is global awareness in preaching as mission in America, or there is no authentic preaching at all. The chief reason is theological, but this interprets Christ in the material and cultural reality. Multinational or transnational companies maximize profits and minimize labor and manufacturing costs by producing goods in Asia, Africa, Latin America, and the Caribbean for consumption there as well as in the rich nations. And the capital enrichment occurs in Europe and North America, where stockholders benefit and where corporate decisions are made. Even the economic level of American churches is partly at the expense of the so-called Third World. The raw materials often cost as much there as in the U.S.A., and the manufactured imports cost a lot more. For example, in many Third World countries, gasoline has been the equivalent of $2 per gallon since the oil crisis of the early 1970s and is over $4 now. Automobiles are almost twice as much as in Europe, and salaries are far lower for most people.

A mission executive who had been a local pastor for nearly thirty years was asked by his fellow pastors what he would do differently if he ever became a local pastor again. He said that he could never again celebrate Holy Communion without mentioning the worldwide nature of the church and the great needs of people in many places. The communion service is a time when the sacrifice of Christ is remembered in its most personal—and therefore most universal—dimensions. The only reason it can mean so much to the individual is because potentially it is meaningful to all.

What Should the Church Be Doing?

A common objection to concern about human rights is the claim that it has nothing to do with religion. It is said to be a social and political matter, not a moral or spiritual one. A statement by The Presbyterian Church of South Korea (PROK) deals with this question and also summarizes the two concerns of this chapter for mission in both a local and global perspective:

The Necessity for Social Proclamations

1. To make known to Christians those things that stand in the way of God's mission, and to increase their concern for social problems;

2. To commend to the people Christ's love and justice, and thus help them to make the right decisions;

3. To help ministers to confront injustice, corruption and social evils, while proclaiming God's kingdom and its righteousness, and give them courage to become involved;

4. To proclaim that mission and service cannot be separated;

5. To overcome the stagnation of the church and its inner conflict, so that it can become the true church. Previously we have insisted on the need to overcome divisions so that the church can be one. In the future, we will put forth our best efforts to make community out of society.

"Area and Problems of Social Proclamations" are then listed by the Korean church for the guidance of the faithful:

1. We will proclaim our ideas with regard to the bringing about of happiness and freedom through the reunification of the country, through increasing world peace and security;

2. Our objection to all dictatorial systems accord-

ing to our understanding of politics, and we will proclaim that the independence of the judiciary must be established;

3. That an end must be put to the misuse of power, which leads to injustice and corruption. We pledge that we will not turn away from social injustice, but that we will challenge and conquer it as soldiers of the cross;

4. That we pledge our church's resources and skills to defeat poverty, humanity's most serious crisis;

5. That we will be out in front in the effort to eradicate pollution, which is a particular threat to the existence of humanity, and that we will promote understanding of this problem by both government and society in general. We will do our best to reduce the gap between the rich and the poor brought about by the deliberate policy of industrialization and urbanization, the gap between rural and urban areas, and between heavy and light industry;

6. That the church will promote democracy in industry in order to bring about peaceful cooperation between labor and management;

7. That the church must be out in front in breaking down the traditional order of obedience, which obstructs the quality of society, bringing discrimination between men and women, and which retains "quaintness" of local color;

8. That we must depend upon reason rather than magic, scientific heritage rather than superstition, sincere effort rather than luck; doing our best to educate society at the same time, mobilize it to enable it to accept change without confusion;

9. While listening to what the younger generation is saying, the church must make proclamations and go forward closing the gap between the generations. The younger generation sees anything from the past as a dismal failure, and sees nothing but the destruction of the world in the approaching future;

10. We must not only pray for the oneness of the church, we must pray for the oneness of humanity, and we must work hard for continuing peace in our country, proclaiming our hope and expectations that God, our Father, will give this desired peace.

Notes

6

A Guide for Liberation Preaching

The biblical story of liberation begins when Israel sees God's action in the Exodus and relates it to the religious consciousness of the covenant and to the blessing of the creation. The result is the Torah, by which the community identifies itself with the honor of God. The people try to achieve justice through a system of laws and precepts, many of them borrowed from nations like Egypt and Babylon, set in the new context of God's covenant.

In spite of the true holiness of the priesthood, piety is sometimes directed toward cultic purity in such a way that it becomes repressive, but that is not its only limitation, as we see in the message of the prophets. There is a constant effort to correct the traditional piety in the interests of liberation. The word and the Spirit create a human response that sets free in many ways, until Paul can write: "For all alike have sinned, and all alike are deprived of the divine splendour, and all are justified by God's free grace alone, through his act of liberation in the person of Christ Jesus" (Rom. 3:23-24, NEB).

This is also the ultimate purpose of preaching. Men and women are prompted to express thanks through generosity and compassion in all their actions and attitudes. Love becomes the attempt to practice justice in every situation and to think of others more than of oneself. It is a sharing of spiritual blessing in every aspect of life.

The practice of liberation is typified in the fruits of the Spirit enumerated by Paul in Galatians 5:22-23: "love, joy, peace, patience, kindness, goodness, faithfulness, gentleness, self-control." The faith of our spiritual ancestors enabled them to overthrow kingdoms, establish justice, and see God's promises fulfilled (Heb. 11:33). This means a freedom to relate in a new way to wives, husbands, children, masters, and slaves—certainly in the limited context of the first century, but all the more liberating because of that context.

The level of sexism and repression in the Bible is nowhere near as intense and dehumanizing as in the surrounding cultures. The Bible points to the overcoming of sexist and repressive injustices, not to their justification. Look at the relation of Jesus to women at every point in the Gospels. Mary and Martha were not to work only in the kitchen! (Luke 10:38-42) Even the very limited recommendations for relations between husbands and wives, the criticism of homosexuality, and the discussion of masters and slaves represent a breakthrough from the self-enclosed and self-perpetuating conditions of that time. Many of the biblical precepts and moral judgments are made in the context of pagan religious practices. This explains the harsh judgments on both homosexual and heterosexual conduct.

Freedom is promised in the Epistle of James (1:25-27, NEB): "But the man [sic! Sexist terms not adapted in these excerpts] who looks closely into the perfect law, the law that makes us *free*, and who lives in its company, does not forget what he hears but acts upon it; and that is the man who by acting will find happiness. A man may think he is religious, but if he has no control over his tongue, he is deceiving himself; that man's religion is futile. The kind of religion which is without stain or fault in the sight of God the Father is this: to go to the help of widows and orphans in their affliction and keep oneself untarnished by the world."

The social implications of faith in Christ are everywhere emphasized in the New Testament: "The man who does not love is still in the realm of death, for everyone who hates his brother is a murderer, and no murderer, as you know, has eternal life dwelling within him. It is by this that we know what love is: that Christ laid down his life for us. And we in our turn are bound to lay down our lives for our brothers. But if a man has enough to live on, and yet when he sees his brother in need shuts up his heart against him, how can it be said that the divine love dwells in him?" (1 John 3:14-17, NEB).

The Practice of a New Freedom

The people to whom we direct our preaching are called to new relationships by the power of God, with one another and with their brothers and sisters of all nations. In our family relationships we must seek what is liberating for each other—that freedom which is in Christ, not license or permissiveness, but the affirmation of personhood before God. Preachers must give one example, at least, by avoiding sexist language. Where "people" is meant instead of *men* that should be made clear in every reading of the Bible or liturgical text. A close guard on our use of sexist language is important today.

Preachers must be advocates of those who suffer. Where else can the responsibility of decision-makers be made clear? The problems of justice in Latin America do not depend on the present U. S. administration, but it must be called upon to press for human rights. The problem in many countries goes back to those who made decisions at Yalta and Potsdam, decisions which eventually isolated Eastern Europe and divided Korea without the advice or consent of anyone directly affected. Where can clarity of judgment come on those in Washington who continued to withhold food and reconstruction aid to Vietnam and whose action resulted in the crisis of the refugees and boat people as well as the tragedy of Kampuchea? And where can judgment come on those who refused to try to understand Ho Chi Minh in 1944 and 1945, who supported the French with money and arms to keep Vietnam divided after Dien Bien Phu, who refused to permit elections to be held in 1956, who always turned a deaf ear to the better counselors, and who contrived to involve us in a horrible and exhausting war in 1965? Why do we have this risk again in Central America and the Caribbean?

A Christology of the History of All Peoples

There are patterns of liberation in other religions to which we must be alert, and these are an expression of God's grace. There is a Christological meaning in *all* peoples' history. In the history of every society there is conflict of power that results in oppression and inhuman treatment. There develops a sector of society that is poor, insecure, victimized by violence, and outcast. These men and women are the humble of the earth, those who do not manage instruments of authority and power, who do not possess land, for whom farming and shepherding is a brutalizing and humiliating attempt to scratch out a meager existence. The meaning of a society is borne by this persecuted and oppressed class of people. The degree of humanity and fulfillment of life within the society is represented by them, not by the privileged and fortunate few. However, this is an ethical judgment; it is not yet Christological.

Jesus himself suffered an apparently meaningless and undeserved death at the hands of uncaring rulers. The Christological significance enters when we see that God is disclosed to the world through the history of Israel in such a way that God is seen to be concerned for all the wretched of the earth. God's judgment falls on those who treat persons like animals. This gives the world the true understanding of injustice. It also gives the world a picture of a truly human and liberating religion, which includes the resurrection of the just!

The suffering of the poor is not in itself redemptive. Nothing can justify it. It is the suffering of Christ, the person Jesus of Nazareth, that is redemptive because it is the source of faith. The saving health of all the nations is in the critical attitude of the poor, a sense of being "poor in spirit." The gospel is addressed to all people, which means it is heard in a sense of solidarity with those in special need. The "poor in spirit" are those who rejoice that the righteousness of God will triumph in the end! It is they who suffer with the poor and who are trying to do something about a more fulfilling life in community for us all.

True piety toward God is not in the praise of omnipotence or the sacrifice of blood offerings and nature's wealth to maintain the "balance" of the universe. It is the recognition of God's revelation and salvation through the Christ, who became the brother of all. We see Christ in the poor because we see the poor in Christ. We see God in the promise of resurrection and new life, for throughout history we see changes and sacrifices that come about on behalf of love and justice.

Because there is a Christological meaning in all peoples' history, we do not conceive the mission of the church to be the maintenance and extension of a Western institution. It means that we are involved in the central dynamic of human history itself. All our concepts of creation and providence, our belief in a personal God, and our trust in the Savior are one with the struggle for a better society, for a more broadly shared prosperity, for true happiness, which the world in our time is calling "liberation." The point is that this history is Christological, not merely sociological, so that liberation entails also the inescapable presence of spiritual anxiety, our common mortality, and God's sure love.

The practice of liberation is to awaken to the fact that Asians, Africans, and Latin Americans have been struggling for independence and various degrees of socialism and enterprise for forty years—ever since five hundred years of colonialism finally came to an end. Our present history is the attempt to overcome the imperialism and violence of our own conquest, which began in Massachusetts and extended to Hawaii and the Philippines. Our economic politics took everything everywhere by force of arms, even though many church and community leaders, missionaries, and laborers opposed it. The "anti-imperialist" party of 1900 is a significant reminder of resistance to plunder.

Someone botched our relations with China in the 1940s and made us supporters, until 1979, of an oppressive regime in Taiwan. Brazil, Chile, Uruguay, and most other Latin American countries were enabled by us to suppress socialist movements, falling under military dictatorship for decades. The churches in these countries called for our attention. Progressive Christians—especially ministers, priests, and nuns—suffered, and still suffer torture, exile, and death. What has been the response of American churches? For the most part, they have reflected the reactionary suspicion and anger of the most conservative elements of the community, and they have condoned the most reprehensible use of their economic and human resources in violence and murder.

The actions and decisions of some governmental leaders have been criminal. If we cannot do anything about the crimes of the past, we can attempt to effect change in the present and the future. Preaching as mission means to help people begin a practice of liberation that can help save the world from unimaginable inhumanity and even from annihilation. Most persons elected to office or raised to high positions are not prepared by their churches to crave peace and to create justice. These leaders prove, as nothing else does, the near sterility of the pulpit since the cold war began, when it comes to politics.

The real religion of America after World War II was anticommunism. Because of this, many thoughtful persons left the church and cannot take it seriously today. Anti-communism is still the most emotional chord in the hearts of our church people. Ministers can only touch it indirectly by seeking to overcome this and every other demonic power through the exorcising and liberating love of Christ. The call of evangelist Billy Graham for a reversal of the arms race shows a decided shift in the understanding of how to be peacemakers.

The catalog of our political failures is not the result of paranoia. It is a positive approach to the church and to American society because it sees the content of religion and the gospel as irrepressible light and freedom. The practice of liberation is a real possibility because the history of the gospel in American society has paralleled the struggle for liberation here. May 1 as a holiday is not of Russian origin. It is the anniversary of the bloody Chicago Haymarket Square repression after the strike over the eight-hour day at the McCormick Harvesting Machine Company in 1886. Like many of our best traditions, May 1 has been surrendered to the Communist world. We downgrade the sacrifices of the past and the role of laborers, even though they are the source of our special freedoms today. How many Pittsburgh schoolchildren learn about the Homestead strike of July, 1892, which was broken up by murderous Pinkerton goon squads and thugs and which retarded the organization of unions in the steel mills for over forty years?

But our people know what is right and fair. The gospel has still been with us in many ways! A new seriousness about the role of preaching, its hard work and its risks, its inspiration and its grace, can make a new impact in American society for the benefit of ordinary people everywhere.

Preaching the practice of liberation is nothing less than calling our people to the realistic implications of the kingdom of God—not in the expectation of changing human nature but in the full knowledge of what human nature is and does here and around the world. It seeks to curb human excesses and to channel its forces for good. It is the hope of a more abundant life.

Toward a New Practice

In the midst of the decade of the 1980s, there is on every hand a call for the teaching of cultural values and the basics of civilized life. Where will these be found if not in a renewed respect for the religious tradition and for its theological inspiration? Do the schools have some resource that we have overlooked? Does the municipal or state political structure embody the healthy spirit of American pluralism? Do the police and courts or the federal government show examples of justice and civic wisdom that should be more widely emulated? Do the professions of medicine and law and engineering—or the whole range of science and technology—demonstrate that educated people have a disinterested philosophy of social ethics and humanistic culture to share with the younger generation? Does the business community, especially in its international manifestations, have an experience of human fellowship and world order that can serve to enlighten the minds and refine the spirits of our compatriots?

The pretentiousness of the effort to teach values lies not only in its irony but in its paternalism. The teaching of values is an experiential exercise in which assent is as important as content, and incentives are as important as penalties. The younger generation needs to learn about the struggles that produced the ballot box and habeas corpus. But they will build their own system of adequate values if they see some real degree of community solidarity, respect for the dignity and rights of all persons, and a concentration of efforts for justice, law enforcement, and peace.

Preaching the gospel is more critical than ever for developing moral discernment and for the cultivation of joy and freedom, for it awakens faith and inspires worship. Since the founding of the first Benedictine abbeys in Europe, the gospel has had a civilizing role in our cultural history. Beginning with a disciplined life, the Benedictines created through daily work well-being for persons and progress in the use of natural resources, agriculture, and crafts. Monks were equally at home with the sciences, philosophy, arts, music, architecture, and industry. They ran the hospice, the mill, the dairy herd, the foundry, the book-copying, and the school as acts of obedience to the kingdom of Christ.

The connection between the true cultural values of our present society and our religious roots is unbreakable. Even secularization is a form of such continuity. Its social motivation is a humanism based on the worth of each person in the total scheme of things. That comes from beyond the goals and the satisfactions of secularism itself.

Preaching as mission can point us to a new practice of liberation in the 1980s:

l. *A new way of relating to persons as co-workers.* As new roles are defined, we can seek a structure of family and marriage that enhances the freedom and responsibility of individuals who care about each other. We can highlight the concern for all members of a neighborhood, the worth of each contribution through daily employment as part of a social whole, and ethical imperatives for teachers, business people, health care workers, and public servants. We can find that we are brothers and sisters in our communities. We can be proud of our different races, the Spanish language, Asian and other ethnic backgrounds, and older citizens.

2. *A new refusal to live under the domination of hate and fear.* We can realize that hate destroys our humanity and that, as Martin Luther King, Jr. said, our struggles for justice need the ingredient of love. No one can build a new society anywhere on hate and fear. No one can build a just public administration on indifference. Love is an expression of friendship for all people, necessary for the pursuit of happiness under *any* system. Non-violence is a sign for the restraint of the powerful, not for limiting the just cause of the oppressed. "Hate is always reactionary," says Padre Ernesto Cardenal.

3. *A new languge that expresses respect.* Sexism and racism have no place in the language of liberated people. Anti-Semitism must be consciously resisted when we read the New Testament. "Socialism" can no longer be a word we fear to use. Homosexuality can be seen in terms of people rather than stereotypes and self-consciousness. References to the poor or to Third World countries that are disparaging or arrogant can be replaced by terms of respect.

4. *A new sense of purpose for our lives.* Liberation from class ideologies and paranoia can give a new conviction of what life is about and the worth of every effort. There can be hope in the future and commitment to the building of com-

munity and peace among all peoples. Our national priorities ought to include what each of us can contribute and also what we consider necessary for a peaceful world.

5. A new resistance to the power of money. A critical attitude toward our anxieties about security, and serenity in the midst of the tensions of consumerism, are important aspects of spiritual freedom. We can seek to curb the power of transnational corporations and support the use of funds for the development of poorer nations in terms of their own people's needs. We can support our church and the ecumenical movement far better than we do, as a sign of our real love for God and of our grasp of God's love for us and for the world.

6. A new definiteness of Faith. We can take more seriously our faith commitment and seek doctrinal clarity on matters that seem important in our heritage. Faith can be centered on the enrichment of human life for all people and on a recognition that God's judgment upon injustice is like a refiner's fire. Trust in eternal life should be a path to generosity. Belonging to the church needs to be seen as a sharp affirmation of the impact of Christ in history and of our discipleship with him in the Spirit.

7. A new political voice as citizens. An analytical spirit that supports democratic institutions and legal norms of human rights is possible for every member of society. Accountability to the people may be expected of not only every elected official, but also of everyone exercising power, including economic power and any decision-making that is based on community assent. Matters of economic justice, environmental safety, and civil rights require constant vigilance and citizen protest.

8. A new sexual continence. The morality of sexual conduct is in need of a new consensus, but it is not only a matter of what is legal and illegal. What is at stake is our view of the person, in relation to all other persons in a hierarchy of intimacy. The male exploitation of females in pornography and pimping is not an expression of sexual love but of love of money, fantasy, and violence. Homosexual and extra-marital love raises questions of relationship and trust as much as any other. Promiscuity is self-contradictory and destructive of character and affection in both homosexual and heterosexual relations. The freedom to be fair and responsible calls for a new examination of the moral life.

9. A new understanding of the true greatness of our country. The practice of liberation is a practice of hope and determination. There is no sincere criticism of democracy that is not in the democratic interests of the people. The greatness of one's country is its capacity to restrain abuses of power by law and to set supreme value on the constitutional rights of citizens. It can only do that by seeking the welfare of other nations as well and by the renunciation of narrow materialism and militaristic propaganda. The true greatness of our country lies in the struggle for freedom in which we Americans have participated and in the relatively open society bequeathed to us and to our children. A new respect for, and solidarity with, the poor people of the whole world is the true patriotism for which we should strive among our own.

10. A new commitment to peace. The escalation of nuclear armaments in the world is not only a danger of unpredictable proportions and unforeseeable contingencies but also a waste of production and resources urgently needed even by our own society. They are a contradiction of elementary human striving. A new commitment to peace does not mean the absence of restraints on aggression or the failure to curb injustices. It means that a new wisdom must be brought to bear on international problems. We must create new interlocking relationships. There must be born among us a new political will for coexistence, for cooperation in the building of a more just international economic order, and for human life together on this planet.

There is no liberating practice more basic to the church of Jesus Christ on the threshold of the twenty-first century than for its members to become nonconformists and activists for *peace*. In the context of moral struggle and the tragic nature of history, this would not be the final word on obedience to the will of God but rather its beginning and presupposition. Our dependence on grace is our independence. Our practice of liberation for justice and peace is the power of hope through the power of God, who is with the people still.

This, then, is at least part of what is needed for preaching the practice of liberation:

1. A new way of relating to persons as co-workers.
2. A new refusal to live under the domination of hate and fear.
3. A new language that expresses respect.
4. A new sense of purpose for our lives.
5. A new resistance to the power of money.
6. A new definiteness of faith.
7. A new political voice as citizens.
8. A new sexual continence.
9. A new understanding of the true greatness of our country.
10. A new commitment to peace.

Appendix

Lectionary Texts with Suggestions for Liberation Preaching

Selections from the Common Lectionary, Year A

(These are a few examples of liberation themes to be found in lectionary readings.)

First Sunday in Advent
Isaiah 2:1-5; Psalm 122;
Romans 13:11-14; Matthew 24:36-44.

The Isaiah passage is memorable for its metaphors for peace: "swords into plowshares, spears into pruning hooks." Peace is a necessary theme for preaching in anticipation of the birth of the Prince of Peace. Longing for peace is the same as the longing for the Messiah and for the coming of God's kingdom in fullness. It is worldwide in scope. It pertains to justice and love as the ways of God. It heralds the birth of Christ as missionary tidings of great joy.

With the Gospel and Epistle readings, the exhortation to *keep watch* is linked with the fulfillment of God's promise in the Nativity. These texts are not historically related to the Christchild, but they are theologically linked to him. Advent becomes not just a time of anticipation and preparing, but one of confidence in the power of God to make God's Word live among us and to be victorious in deliverance from violence, sin, and death. It is the beginning of a new time that radically changes the course of our lives, breaking in on us in a way we could not have planned. Instead of saying, "Nothing will ever make any difference," we can say, "Here is God's glory revealed in Jesus Christ." We are enabled to trust that our efforts for peace and justice are worthwhile because that glory has endured the struggle and has enlightened our own hearts.

Second Sunday in Advent
Isaiah 11:1-10; Psalm 72:1-8;
Romans 15:4-13; Matthew 3:1-12.

Isaiah sees the peacable kingdom of the One whom God will send—a theology of the total environment! The blessing of God is for the whole world, every people, even animals. The reign of Christ in our hearts is meant to serve all who suffer, all who are poor, all victims of oppression. The kingdom of God brings unconditional reconciliation and an end to every kind of enmity. This is not universalistic utopianism. It is a disposition of faith, with roots in the biblical perception of the Creator and of the value of the whole creation.

Jesus is seen as belonging to the lineage of Jesse because everything about him is rooted in the culture of the Jews. War among nations, injustice toward the poor, and the tragedies of nature are not inevitable and are to be overcome eventually by the love of God! Therefore, people of faith must live in the real world without cynicism and share in the signs of active hope without illusions.

For this reason, John the Baptist has a place in Advent. He represents the tradition of the prophets like Isaiah, both in his

Jewish context and in the universalism of his proclamation. The beginning time of the Christchild is also the end time for those who believe. When the kingdom of God is near, there is judgment on sin and liberation for the whole created order.

Third Sunday in Advent
Isaiah 35:1-10; Psalm 146:5-10;
James 5:7-10; Matthew 11:2-11.

The signs of the messianic fulfillment of the grace of God are linked to the healings of Jesus in the response Jesus gave to John's disciples. This is a clue to the meaning of all the New Testament miracles. They show not a supernatural power bestowed on a few to prove the superiority of their religion, but the coming of the messianic age promised by God and for so long anticipated in faith.

These signs are identified with Isaiah 35 and the sufferings of the parched land, the weak and fearful who hope only in the God of justice and mercy, the terror from beasts of prey, and the vulnerability of those who are blind, deaf, and lame. Assurance is given in the acts of Jesus that the life and condition of each person is of infinite worth and that God's word of judgment and liberation is not in vain. This is the meaning of Christ's coming, of Advent.

Patience is good counsel, of course. But the vision of the Lord's resurrection has enabled the New Testament writers to present the birth of Jesus of Nazareth in the language of the last judgment and of God's final victory of love and peace. For this reason, the prophets of the coming kingdom are also the prophets of the coming King.

Fourth Sunday in Advent
Isaiah 7:10-16; Psalm 24;
Romans 1:1-7; Matthew 1: 18-25.

The young girl or virgin will conceive and bear a son whose name will be Immanuel ("God with us"). Paul says this in every line of his great theological letter to the Romans, and Matthew writes the tender story for the beginning of his theological Gospel. Isaiah was talking to Ahaz about a "sign." So is Matthew as he relates the magnificent passage to the person of Jesus. So is Paul as he sees the same power of God in the Resurrection.

The sign means something only to those people who look upon it as a sign! What is signified is the important thing, and in these three texts faith is concerned with God's involvement in human history at the point of people's greatest need. This is true of all people and of all suffering and of all love. It is true of Jesus, not as an idea or an attitude, but in the concreteness of Jewish history and literature, the work of theological poets and priests.

The result is Christmas as the celebration of a community formed around his teaching and his spiritual power. This power becomes worldwide, leads to faith and obedience in people of all nations, as Paul says, and sets in motion the mission of hope and love in his name. Immanuel, God with us, is a liberating force that changes history and humanity in countless ways. Advent joins brothers and sisters throughout the world.

Christmas, I

Isaiah 9:2-7; Psalm 96;
Titus 2:11-14; Luke 2:1-20.

These texts are so rich in rejoicing and praise that our preaching can begin at any point, with any figure, even with any word. A good commentary will provide helpful insights and prevent straying from the central message that God intentionally "sets us free from all wickedness" (Titus 2:14, NEB). God makes us a new kind of community through the child born to suffer the oppression of humankind.

Notice the repeated exultations that refer to peace, justice, truth, deliverance, the light of hope, and trust in the future, proclaiming the glory of God and good news to the whole earth. The angels represent the spiritual power of the Christmas event. They represent what is normally visible only to eyes of faith, like the poetry of Isaiah, the promise of Psalm 96, and the conviction of first-century Christians that grace has been lavished in Christ for the healing of all humankind.

Liberation is concrete and practical, upsetting social and political bondage eventually, because it is a renovation of the spirit and the resurrection of life in God, claiming dignity and rights for all people. "All the people" (Luke 2:10, RSV) or "the whole people" (NEB) means that the vast number of poor and outcast, those with handicapping conditions of all kinds, even the bearers of the most heavy and tragic burdens, are given "great joy." The end of their deprivation and despair is in sight through the will of God and the love manifested in Jesus Christ. Our own commitment is enlisted in that gift!

Christmas, II
Isaiah 62:6-7, 10-12; Psalm 97;
Titus 3:4-7; Luke 2:8-20.

It may be well to start with Titus, for this is what the church must not fail to teach and to proclaim: The Creator God, full of kindness and generosity toward the whole world, forgives and saves through Jesus Christ, putting us in touch with the inner depths of our lives by the power of the Holy Spirit. We are "justified by grace" in order that we may have hope for eternal life.

But we must not fall into the very heresy which Titus condemns: spiritualizing the hope of faith. The Savior is the liberator described in Isaiah, one who brings in judgment, justice, love, and peace in a definite future. Eternal life is not entry into a distant paradise, but life in the coming kingdom of God that both transforms and transcends this world. To Christians of the New Testament, immortality is to live now and forever with the resurrected Christ in the lovingkindness of God, who created the world and who is not indifferent to the evils and injustices of history.

Read Psalm 97 again, and remember that this is the God of Jesus, who grants peace to those with whom he is "well pleased." *Eudokia* is a term for those people of whatever religion, culture, and history upon whom the favor of God rests because of their love, compassion, and service, even before the birth of Jesus. This is the theological ground for dialogue with people of other faiths or ideologies. Some who have never heard the gospel fulfill God's will better than those who have. The Spirit blows where it will, and grace is the true nature of God.

The poem of Isaiah 62 shows the purpose of God in its most reassuring form, when Forsaken and Desolate become My Delight and Married. How much depth of faith would be discovered at Christmas if the texts of Isaiah were studied in detail and made the subject of meditation in the church!

First Sunday After Christmas
Isaiah 63:7-9; Psalm 111;
Hebrews 2:10-18; Matthew 2:13-15, 19-23.

We should never ignore the political massacre at Bethlehem! Matthew 2:16-18 should be included in this lesson. It is too important to overlook because it is the presence of the cross within the Christmas story.

Rather than an idealistic children's story, Christmas is a prologue to everything that follows in the life and death of Jesus, interpreted through faith in the resurrection appearances and their call to the church to preach the gospel to the ends of the earth. The official terrorism of Herod's mercenaries must be kept before the church as a reminder of the similar victims throughout history and frequently in our own time. Where is it happening right now, and which side are we on? The irony is that many church members are caught by surprise when they encounter brutality, evil, and death. In fact, the life of Jesus and his teaching of the kingdom of God are fully incarnated in the suffering and oppression of the human condition.

Our concern for liberation is to challenge the philosophical idealism that makes the faith individualistic, private, and conventional. Since the attempt to exterminate European Jews in the twentieth century, the crucifixion can never be abstracted from reality, nor can we be presumptuous about God's care. What is more significant than the family of Jesus, like that of Moses, having to hide the baby? Refugees from oppression and fugitives from injustice and murder! We have overlooked the role of Africa (Egypt) in the Christmas story, but it is there from the beginning.

The Letter to the Hebrews sees liberation from the fear of death and from the power of the devil as a release from a servile life. Think of this in practical terms as it relates to the people being persecuted in the first century or this one.

Epiphany
Isaiah 60:1-6; Psalm 72:1-14;
Ephesians 3:1-12; Matthew 2:1-12.

Epiphany means the true disclosure of God's glory in Jesus Christ. Therefore, the Ephesians passage speaks of God's secret purpose, the hidden wisdom and unfathomable riches, both spiritual and historical, centered in the glorified man on the cross. This shows the radical importance of Jesus in our understanding of God and in our relationship to one another. This hymn of faith does not celebrate what is self-evident in the world through experience, but what is promised in the church through the Spirit. It is a liberation from the alienating powers that always seem to win!

The Asian priests who confirm the coming glory follow the star to his place of birth, and their homage is a tribute not to the superiority of Christianity, but to the triumph and grace of God revealed in love for the universe.

Isaiah's vision of the epiphany of God's glory in the new Jerusalem is linked with the coming of foreign nations to bow the knee and present gifts as signs of obedience. The "wise men" become kings in the popular imagination of early Christians. They even acquire names and represent the different races of humankind in the Epiphany dramas of the Middle Ages. Gold, frankincense, and myrrh are characteristic of sacred offerings and divine anointing from the time of Moses (Exodus 30). Here, Matthew combines the particularity of scripture and the universality of creation by bringing the Gentile astrologers to the Jewish scribes in order to find Bethlehem of Judea.

The Psalm shows the heart of this glory to be revealed: peace and justice for all the people, above all for the poor and the oppressed. The world mission of the church is shown here not by the apostles' going out to the ends of the earth but by the world coming to the infant Jesus with its own recognition of blessing.

First Sunday After Epiphany
Isaiah 42:1-9; Psalm 29;
Acts 10:34-42; Matthew 3:13-17.

Again the emphasis on all creation and the blessing of all peoples! This is portrayed in two ways: mercy toward the infirm and the liberation of captives, on the one hand, and the humble submission of the mighty, on the other. Everywhere in scripture there are signs of the coming kingdom of God. There are now no "favorites," Jew or Gentile, before God, writes Peter, the man of eschatological visions—not because "God loves everyone" but because God loves everyone else the way God loves the Jews. The same providence is shown in their creation, calling for respect and empathy toward every history, culture, and religion. The same judgment falls upon their sin of arrogance, exploitations, idolatry, personal hatred, and alienating superstitions or ideologies. The same liberation is offered to all in the forgiveness, renewal, love, and hope of the cross.

Thus Epiphany is a proclamation about the unity of humankind through the Gospel. Epiphany expresses the wholeness and destiny of all things in the unity of Father, Son, and Holy Spirit. The Creator is present in the world through real forgiveness and the power of love. The baptism of Jesus shows the human side of the divine—the relativity of Jewish culture and traditions to which Jesus gives assent through John the Baptist. It shows the unconditional worth of the sacrifice of God's beloved for every time and place.

Second Sunday After Epiphany
Isaiah 49:1-7; Psalm 40:1-11;
1 Corinthians 1:1-9; John 1:29-34.

Kings and princes, deliverance and lovingkindness, Lamb of God who takes away the sin of the world—Epiphany is the explosion of Christ's meaning for the whole world. Remember the difficult times in which all these hopeful, extravagant texts were written, recited, copied, and recopied—generation after generation! What is so unlikely as these confident affirmations? They came so often from a small band facing persecution or martyrdom.

The words of Paul remind us that their declarations are true because they contain the living seeds of the future. The word of God is in them, and they are called the word of God because of their spiritual power. They bring about a reality that becomes part of the experience of the people.

The season of Epiphany announces the beginning of a new year because it brings the timeless teaching and faith of the church! This is the gospel that gives the church its love, courage, and joy, but that also transcends the church and judges or renews it from afar. Jesus is Lord! But make no mistake about what his lordship, in the beatitudes and parables, encounters in the streets or homes of Judea and in the cross. Jesus is Lord! But hearts are opened by grace to receive that gift in ways that we cannot foresee. Jesus is Lord! But Paul reminds us that "the Day" is somewhere out ahead of us. It is God's day, and God has called us to share in it—now through firmness, and then in fullness.

To face the sufferings and struggles of our existence, both privately and in society, with the certainty that the poor and lonely have good reason to hope and everything to look forward to, is a liberating act, the culmination of what it means to be a human being. As Pasternak writes, "We must remain faithful to immortality." The Word of God took on our humanity so that our humanity could reach its fullest dimensions in our becoming friends and children of God.

Third Sunday After Epiphany
Isaiah 9:1-4; Psalm 27:1-6;
I Corinthians 1:10-17; Matthew 4:12-23.

In the context of darkness and oppression, the theme of light and salvation is claimed for Jesus! Against the foreign power that annexed the land of Zebulun and Naphtali in the eighth century B.C. comes the prophet's word of hope and trust. It is incorporated into the Gospel of Matthew at the point where John the Baptist is arrested by Herod. The shadow of death and the heavy burden of military domination are not only contrasted with the dawning of God's deliverance, but are declared to be vanquished by it.

How many people of faith, in prison or faced by injustice and even torture, have been sustained by Psalm 27!

The Lord is my light and my salvation;
whom shall I fear?
The Lord is the stronghold of my life;
of whom shall I be afraid?

In a most personal way, love for God and the consciousness of divine goodness and grace can encourage us in any hardship. Because of the witness of many people, that must be said. Some are strengthened more than others, but where there is faith all are helped to some extent.

The first half of the twentieth century will be noted for its great theologians. The second half will be remembered for poems, letters, songs, and meditations by the persecuted. These are prophets of liberation for a more humane world—priests and pastors, nuns and lay workers, student leaders and community organizers, labor leaders and human rights advocates, peacemakers and hard-working parents claiming a better future for their children.

The message of Jesus that shed light in the darkness was, "The kingdom of heaven is at hand" and "Come with me." Both phrases say the same thing. He gathered a community to carry his light forever. Epiphany does not lead us to a Christian system of religion nor to a Christian form of philosophy but to Jesus Christ.

We are accustomed to the call for unity made by Paul in 1 Corinthians. That unity is found in Jesus Christ, the Word of God made light and life. Paul tells us that the community is based on the fact of Christ on his cross. That is the meeting point for Christians, and there is no other focus for faith.

The grace of God is known in many ways by many peoples, but for the church it is always consonant with the crucifixion. That must have its full weight among us, Paul tells us, and that is why Epiphany is a time of glory. We celebrate the salvation in Christ that makes us part of God's reign forever, the salvation that resists and endures the forces of evil and death for ourselves and for all people.

Last Sunday After Epiphany
Exodus 24:12-18; Psalm 2:7-11;
2 Peter 1:16-21; Matthew 17:1-9.

What a burst of glory leads us to the end of the Epiphany season! The children of Israel stand in awe before Mt. Sinai. The wrath and triumph of Psalm 2 manifests itself over God's holy hill, Zion. The narrative of Jesus' transfiguration proclaims the fulfillment of the law (Moses) and the prophets (Elijah). The witness of 2 Peter is that faith in Christ is not the result of religious intuition, but of the power and word of the living God.

The glory that clothes Jesus of Nazareth is God's own presence. There is nothing arbitrary in the memory of the beginnings of a people under God, delivered from oppression in Egypt and liberated by justice and hope in the covenant of

Moses. The same glory revealed here judges and redeems the world. All of these scripture texts look forward to the end time—not to a bleak abyss of human failure but to the love and righteousness of God.

Epiphany closes with a vision of the coming kingdom of God, in which the crucified rabbi and prophet is Lord of all. That kingdom is with us now whenever the Holy Spirit is at work through acts of love and mercy, always pointing to the future and giving us trust in God. The center of this vision of faith and the glory that brings joy and peace is Christ in all of his teaching and calling and suffering. In the most personal commitment and mystical devotion, or in the most political and economic of our struggles and burdens, the companion of our way is Jesus. The ultimate deliverance from evil is the abiding grace of God that is seen in him. The glory of God in Jesus Christ is the ecstasy of hope in the apostolic community and the motivation of its mission in the whole world.

Ash Wednesday
Joel 2:1-2, 12-17a; Psalm 51:1-12;
2 Corinthians 5:20b—6:2 (3-10); Matthew 6:1-6, 16-21.

"Be reconciled to God!" says Paul, "the day of deliverance has dawned." The beginning of Lent brings us to the time of the Atonement. What does it mean today to say that Christ died for our sins? It means that our sins are not final. They no longer have power over us. In whatever direction they lie, from the imperfections and idiosyncrasies of each human being to the massive greed and vicious cruelty of social systems, they do not nullify our best efforts. It is not we who overcome them, but it is Christ who releases us from them. Liberation is one of the meanings of forgiveness in the New Testament.

What release is there in the new attitude and practice that repentance and forgiveness represent? It is the liberation of a new beginning, the yoke of Christ that is his mission instead of our burden of guilt and remorse, release of people from the wrong ways and the brutal forces that would recruit them to destroy their neighbors. In keeping with this season, the texts speak of our spiritual duty before God, and they call for inward humility rather than outward form.

This is not to judge ourselves better than others or to secularize Lent by reference to mundane struggles. It is to enter into a time of deep appreciation of the cross! Nothing more radically confronts us with the suffering and despair of millions in our world, nothing more directly calls attention to uncaring and cynical affluence than the same crucified Savior who brings us to mercy and new life through faith. There is no enmity left in the heart touched by God's grace—neither enmity toward other people nor enmity toward the goodness and hope that God brings. There is no distance from God to be covered by our repentance except the acceptance of God's word of life in a spirit of adoration.

First Sunday in Lent
Genesis 2:4b-9, 15-17, 25—3:7; Psalm 130;
Romans 5:12-19; Matthew 4:1-11.

The first Sunday in Lent introduces the Bible's awareness of sin. Human beings are responsible for yielding to temptations that separate them from one another, from their own contentment, and from God. The story of Adam and Eve does not account for human depravity but for human fallibility and the sense of guilt that life accumulates because of our imperfections. The story is simply an attempt to explain why things are the way they are in a world God has created, a world of goodness and potential harmony. In spite of our good intentions, a kind of seductive power comes between us and our moral judgment, which is faulty from the start. The more perceptive we become about God's will for our personal lives and for the state of the world, the more disappointing our efforts seem to become. In the cases of brutal abuse and systems of injustice and exploitation, the power of evil becomes dominant and degrading. That is why we call it "diabolical." We should take all the literature about Faust very seriously.

And we should pay closer heed to the description of evil in Martin Luther's hymn "A Mighty Fortress Is Our God."

From Psalm 130 comes the cry out of the depths—*De Profundis*. Both as sinner and sinned against, the person of faith discovers the hope of mercy and the taste of liberation. That's what faith in God means.

Paul sees the parallel between our limitations and God's grace. Christ is more determinative for the world than is any temptation. It is his power, not our own, that unites us with God and with one another. The temptation that he endures in the Gospel is the overcoming of temptation for us all. We derive our freedom from him. We boast not of our morality but of his sacrifice. This has the particular value of freeing us from pretensions or hypocrisy regarding racism, class consciousness, revulsion at certain aspects of the human condition, and rationalizations about conditions in the Third World or about poverty in the inner city. There is one characteristic form of modern Protestantism that emerges during Lent—the more or less conscious self-righteousness that trivializes sin, making it seem that Lent has no special meaning for us. Our greatest temptation is weak faith in God's forgiveness and peace.

Second Sunday in Lent

Genesis 12:1-4a (4b-8); Psalm 33:18-22;
Romans 4:1-5 (6-12), 13-17; John 3:1-17 or Matthew 17:1-9.

The covenant with Abraham and the passage from Romans are classic sources for the Protestant teaching of "justification by faith." This is not the only characteristic of our relation to God, whatever our culture or religion, but it is the key to that which is most easily forgotten—that we do not ultimately earn our way to God by merit of any kind. The crucifixion of Jesus is seen by Paul as the breakthrough of God's acceptance, in which the transforming power is known and given by faith alone.

Nicodemus was so near and yet so far! Are we not a little like that ourselves? How very difficult it is to take deeply into our souls the passage from John 3:16-17. This is not triumphalistic. This is not a more difficult version of the law. This is not a form of proselytism. It is the turning from concentration on ourselves to the freedom of a new spirit.

The giving of this sacrifice *for the world* is too much to contemplate. I may see it from one side and say that it does not concern my private life. Or I may view it from the other side and say that it includes even those who are most deprived and afflicted in the immense slums and refugee camps of the world. "God so loved the world . . ." Is my accountability for that world commensurate with my understanding of the love implied in this text? Do I realize that, whether or not I can conceptualize these teachings of the church, this is the true message of the church for all time?

The church, with all of its divisions and shortcomings, has proved over and over the centrality of Jesus Christ in preserving human identity in history. Historical processes sweep whole populations in their wake, but the person who is justified by faith, and not by any other workings of the self or of society, maintains the witness of God's own nature in the world. The atonement serves as a point of reference to keep us open to the possibility that our self-estimate is not shared by everyone, that our way of looking at the world is grossly unfair to people whose main need is to try to survive, and that our religious intuition is not a private satisfaction, but a goad to action for the sake of others.

Notes

1. Reinhold Niebuhr, *Moral Man and Immoral Society*. Scribner's, 1936.

2. John Bartlett (ed.), *Familiar Quotations*, Fourteenth Edition. Little, Brown & Company, 1968, p. 1024.

3. David G. Marr (ed.), *Phan Boi Chau's Prison Notes*. Ohio University Press, 1978, p. 14.

4. From a newsletter.

5. George A. Buttrick et al (eds.), *The Interpreter's Bible*. Abingdon Press, 1952, vol V, p.680.

6. Statement in newsletter by Southeast Asia Institute for Liturgy and Music, St. Andrew's Theological Seminary, Quezon City, Philippines.

Notes

Notes

Notes

Notes